God's
Twentieth Century
Pioneer

Volume I

A compilation of some of the
writings of A. J. Tomlinson

White Wing Publishing House
Cleveland, Tenn.
1962

Introduction

With the advent of the twentieth century has come an age unparalleled and almost unimagined in preceeding age of time. Man has achieved beyond his greatest expectations. The pioneers of the past in the diverse areas of life envisioned and hoped for an age comparable to our age but who can say they truly believed it would come?

The spiritual pioneer whom this book is presenting by way of his own written words did envision, did hope, and most of all, did truly believe the day would come when God's people the world around would seek to find spiritual unity within the Church of God of the Bible. Today, with the twentieth century a little more than half spent, an urgent and increasingly demanding cry has arisen throughout Christendom—a cry for UNITY! Religious leaders of many theologies urge the universal acceptance of one God . . . and one Church for all. In truth, the present trend is toward theoretical unity. But because he believed the day would come when the magistracy of churches and the hearts of men alike would seek spiritual unity, A. J. Tomlinson sought and found the Church of God in the opening years of this, the twenieth century.

GOD'S TWENTIETH CENTURY PIONEER presents a compilation of the writings of the late A. J. Tomlinson, former General Overseer of the Church of God of Prophecy. Of him it has been said, "It seemed that every drop of blood in his veins, every pulsation of his heart and every fiber of his being was dedicated to God and His Church!" This unshakable dedication led A. J. Tomlinson through conflict to great victories, through opposition to glorious achievements.

A. J. Tomlinson was reared to manhood in the state of Indiana during an era when America was experiencing a great spiritual awakening. He was not converted, however, until shortly after his marriage to Mary Jane Taylor in 1889, at the age of twenty-three. He turned almost immediately to the avid study of the Word of God. As a result of his study, a genuine crisis arose in his life—what church to join? A thorough search of the Scriptures led him ultimately to the conviction that there existed but one Church in the sight of God, the Bible Church, and he determined to find it.

A. J. Tomlinson's search led him from Indiana to the wilderness counties of western North Carolina. There he served as an agent for the American Bible Society and as a minister of the gospel, filling pulpits of various congregations upon invitation. Eventually, he met to worship with a small group of people in Cherokee County, North Carolina, who called themselves, "The Holiness Church at Camp Creek." Impressed with their desire to follow the precepts of the Bible, rightly divided, using the New Testament as their only rule of faith and practice, A. J. Tomlinson felt his search was ended. On June 13, 1903, after an early morning prayer, this spiritual pioneer spoke his heartfelt conviction to his Christian brothers and sisters who unanimously consented to set in motion the functioning of the Church of God of the Bible. Little did the group realize how significantly this inspired act corresponded with Isaiah's prophecy concerning the Church "Arise, shine; for thy light is come, and the glory of the Lord is risen upon thee." Isaiah 60:1.

The "glory of the Lord" hovered resolutely over the Church as each year brought new proof of growth. In the year 1910, the Church elected to choose a General Overseer for the various established congregations. A. J. Tomlinson was chosen. Re-elected yearly until 1914, he was then chosen permanently to fill this position in the Church, which he did until his death on October 2, 1943.

During the years in which the late A. J. Tomlinson served as General Overseer of the Church of God of Prophecy, he was ever busily engaged in the propagation of the gospel through the medium of mighty words—spoken and written. This book is the first in a series to feature articles of spiritual pertinence written by this powerful man of God in the interim of his General Overseership. No more appropriate decade could be found for its publication than this. The ecclesiastical world cries for UNITY. "One God, one faith, one mind, and one Church for all!" was the underlying theme which consistently propelled the life work of A. J. Tomlinson, God's Twentieth Century Pioneer!

Sermon Titles

False Teachings

That we mention this as a distinct doctrine may not occasion any great degree of surprise, but to find it unconsciously taught and practiced in these last days might be rather astonishing to some, especially as it may be pointed out in such unexpected places.

There are many doctrines taught in these days, but none to my knowledge is designated as Balaam's Doctrine. But this does not say that such a doctrine does not exist. Modern names are used to express old theories. We are told that one of the old heathen religions now takes a modern name as it is introduced into this country by Mary Baker Eddy, viz., "Christian Science."

This is a time to be particular and careful lest one should become tainted or marred by some false doctrine or delusive spirit and thus be disqualified for the rapture. God, in His infinite wisdom and goodness, has given us His Holy Word and in it is the instructions necessary for our spiritual welfare here in this world and our eternal happiness in the world to come.

Although Balaam evidently had some notoriety before, the first time his name is mentioned in history is where Balak, king of the Moabites, called on him to curse Israel. It is very probable that Balaam was a descendant from Abraham by his second wife, Keturah.

It is evident that Balaam was regarded by his people as a mighty man of God. His doctrine was known by the king, for when he called Balaam to curse Israel, he said, "For I wot that he whom thou blessest is blessed, and he whom thou cursest is cursed." (Num. 22:6) In the history concerning this man it shows that Balaam had communication with God, and that he regarded Him as his God. He declared that he could not go beyond the word of the Lord, his God, to do less or more.

He is further represented in history as practicing divination which thing is spoken of as an abomination to God. (Deut. 18:10-12) He is further represented as an enchanter which also made him an abomination to the Lord. When Balaam was slain the record shows he was called a soothsayer. (Josh. 13:22)

Through the counsel of this man, the children of Israel joined themselves unto Baalpeor and bowed down to the gods of Moab and committed fornication with the Midianitish women. The anger of the Lord was kindled against Israel for this, and 24,000 of them died of the plague that was sent on them.

It is conjectured that Balaam's doctrine was so attractive and fascinating that its influence was almost, if not wholly, irresistible. This conclusion is drawn from the fact that Zimri, an Israelite, brought a Midianitish woman right into the camp, in the sight of Moses and all the congregation, while they were weeping for sorrow over the matter. If he had not been strongly influenced by Balaam's doctrine and peculiar power, he certainly would not have had the courage to commit such a daring deed.

This doctrine of Balaam and the effect it had on the children of Israel was such an offense to God that His wrath was only appeased when Zimri and Cozbi, the Midianitish woman, were both slain. God compliments Phinehas, who slew them, in the very highest terms saying, he "hath turned my wrath away from the children of Israel, while he was zealous for my sake among them, that I consumed not the children of Israel in my jealousy. Wherefore say, Behold, I give unto him my covenant of peace: And he shall have it, and his seed after him, even the covenant of an everlasting priesthood; because he was zealous for his God, and made an atonement for the children of Israel." (Num. 25:11-13) To more fully show His hatred toward Balaam and his doctrine (because the record shows that Balaam was the cause of the trespass, Num. 31:16), God orders Moses to vex the Midianites and smite them (Num. 25:17), and avenge the children of Israel of the Midianites. (Num. 31:2) In this battle Balaam was slain with the sword. (Num. 31:8)

Now that Balaam had a particular doctrine is shown in the message to the pastor and church Pergamos. (Rev. 2:12-14) While the pastor was a good man, and held to the faith of Jesus under the most trying circumstances, yet the Lord had a few things against him, among which was "Because thou hast there them that hold the doctrine of Balaam." The record goes on to state that he taught Balak to cast a "stumblingblock before the children of Israel," and also shows that they taught Israel to eat things sacrificed unto idols, and to commit fornication.

It is plainly seen that this same Balaam doctrine was introduced in the church at Pergamos in the gospel era, 1,548 years after it had appeared in Israel just before the death of Moses. The Lord shows the same displeasure toward it, but this time blames the pastor of the church for allowing it to exist among his members. His wrath is again kindled against the doctrine and those that held to it and the one who allowed it to exist. He accused this pastor of a crime which could only be eliminated by repentance. Then He told him if he did not repent (which infers that this doctrine must be exterminated from his congregation), God Himself would fight against them that held to the abominable doctrine with the sword of His mouth.

Seeing how God's anger was kindled against this doctrine every time it made its appearance, we readily conclude we are on safe footing when we say He would be just as strongly opposed to it should it make its appearance again. Arriving at this conclusion, it behooves us as God's people to be on the watchtower for fear we might be tolerating the very thing that God hates.

This doctrine has five distinct qualities that should claim our attention.

First. It is fascinating.
Second. It despises government.
Third. It is a stumblingblock.
Fourth. It teaches to eat things sacrificed to idols.

Fifth. It teaches to commit fornication.

We will consider these characteristics in the order named.

FASCINATING

Webster defines the word "fascinate" thusly: "To influence the mind or will as if by enchantment; bewitch; captivate; to exercise a bewitching or captivating power." This is the very thing that caught the Israelites and caused them to err and thus courted the displeasure of God. It had such influence over them that they could scarcely extricate themselves from its cruel grasp when once it had them enfolded in its coils. It was beautiful because it always honored God as being its foundation. Call attention to the first answer Balaam gave to the elders of Moab who came to him as messengers when Balak sent to call him to curse Israel, "Lodge here this night, and I will bring you word again, as the LORD shall speak unto me." (Num. 22:8) How much does that sound like a true man of God would do?

DESPISES GOVERNMENT

That this doctrine despises government is shown by the way Israel yielded to its influence in the face of God-given laws that forbade intermingling with other nations and their gods. The influence over them was so strong, that, right in the face of God, His laws, and Moses with all of his objections and warning, this continued until 24,000 people perished under God's wrath. That it despises government is shown by Peter and Jude, both of whom mention the Balaam doctrine in connection with those who despise government. (2 Peter 2:10; Jude 8:13)

STUMBLING BLOCK

That it is a stumbling block is plainly shown in Revelation 2:14. The doctrine is the cause, for Balaam taught Balak to cast a stumbling block before Israel. This signifies that Balak would not have been able to do what he did had it not been for the teaching (doctrine) of Balaam. Balak thought Balaam was the great power of God, just like the people of Samaria thought Simon was the great power of God. Indeed Balaam recognized God in all the delusive actions he performed before Balak. This is, no doubt, what caught Israel, because he always represented himself as being "led of the Lord." Having, on the face of it, the name of God, and its constituents claiming to be led of the Lord is what makes it such a dangerous stumbling block. That which is, or looks to be, the nearest right, yet not right, is the most apt to deceive those who want to be right.

THINGS OFFERED TO IDOLS

Right in the face of Acts 14:29, that doctrine taught to eat things sacrificed to idols. "That you abstain from meats offered to idols." It is evident that Paul had to contend with some who were influenced by this doctrine when he wrote and advised them to have nothing to do with meats offered to idols, for the sake of the weaker brethren who accounted it as sin against Christ to sit at meat in the idol's temple. This doctrine carries with it a self-willed disposition. "I'm going to do what the Lord shows me, whether it pleases folks or not." I have often heard this and similar expressions, but never thought of it at the time in connection with the Balaam doctrine.

FORNICATION

The fifth and last characteristic of this doctrine is that it teaches to commit fornication. Of course it has its slick, magical way to do it, until the victim is innocently deceived and wholly in the dark. Zimri, the character above referred to, was so duped by its wily influence that he brought the Midianitish woman into the camp of Israel and took her into one of the tents right in the presence of Moses and the congregation. It is the Balaam doctrine that leads into "free loveism." It is the Balaam doctrine that is followed when men and women get to kissing each other in obedience, as they say, to Paul and Peter where they teach to greet each other with a kiss. It carries them on into more daring deeds of sin and vice and all the time declares "the Lord led me."

Peter, as well as Revelation 2:14, shows that this doctrine comes right into the Church and takes hold of those who may be very spiritual. Notice, he states that they have forsaken the right way as if they have once been in the right way. (2 Peter 2:15) The first description of them, as he gives it, is that they refuse to recognize government. They say haughtily, "I'm going to let the Lord lead me. I don't expect to be governed by man. I'll do so and so if the Lord shows me. The Lord showed me to do this, and I'm going to do it whether anybody likes it or not." Peter says they are presumptuous, self-willed and not afraid to speak evil of dignities (those in authority). (2 Peter 2:10) Peter shows further that they are spots and blemishes, sporting themselves with their own deceivings, while they feast with you. Then they will come right into the midst of the true worshippers, and appear to be the most spiritual of any, while they boast of how the Lord has led them and revealed to them such great things. Their testimonies will sound like a real child of God, but you can soon locate them when they reject or show that they despise government or authority.

Peter further describes them, saying, "Having eyes full of adultery, and that cannot cease from sin; beguiling unstable souls: and heart they have exercised with covetous practices; cursed children: Which have forsaken the right way, and are gone astray, following the way of Balaam the son of Bosor, who loved the wages of unrighteousness." (2 Peter 2:14, 15)

THE LORD SHOWS

Please notice he says "they are gone astray, following the way of Balaam." What was the way of Balaam? Turn to the record and you will see that he would not go at first, even at the call of the king who had the highest authority, unless the Lord should speak unto him. The record shows that he had a conversation with God who said, "Thou shalt not go with them; thou shalt not curse the people." So he told the princes, after he arose next morning, that "The Lord refuseth to give me leave to go with you."

After this, Balak sent other princes more honorable than the first. Balaam had them to tarry overnight, "that I may know what the Lord will say to me more." The record shows another conversation between this diviner and God and the Lord told him to go with the men. Notice that first God told him not to go, and now He tells him to go. The next thing we notice is that God's anger was kindled against Balaam because he went. Then we read that the angel of the Lord told him to go with the men. So Balaam tried twice to curse Israel and finally said, "Surely there is no enchantment against Jacob, neither is there any divination against Israel."

I have already shown that a diviner and an enchanter were an abomination to God, and Balaam acknowledges in the above statement that he is both, and was doing his very best to divine and enchant against Israel. Peter says that people who despise and reject government are following the way of Balaam. The record shows that God told Balaam not to go, then the angel finally told him to go, and he went and tried to divine and enchant against Israel. All this time, according to the Word of God, he was an abomination in the sight of God! Yet he seemed to be especially careful for God to show him everything he did.

Now listen! I once knew a man who lived in Sweetwater, Tennessee. He claimed he was sanctified. He told me that the Lord told him he would have to quit using tobacco before He would sanctify him. He did quit it and was sanctified. Afterwards he said the Lord showed him to use tobacco and he could still retain his sanctification. This is one instance where a man was following in the way of Balaam. That is a good illustration of Balaam's doctrine. Another case: A gentleman once said the Lord showed him that sanctification was an instantaneous experience obtained subsequent to justification. He claimed the experience and preached it that way a number of years. When the "Finished Work" doctrine came before him, he claimed the Lord showed him that justification and sanctification came at the same time.

The Balaam doctrine emphasizes such expressions as "the Lord shows," and "the Lord leads," and "the Spirit directs,"

and yet the showing is one thing one time and an opposite
or contrary thing at another time, and shows the lack of sta-
bility just like Peter says, and rejects and despises government. At the same time those affected by it seem to
be the most loving people you ever saw. Peter says further
of them, "These are wells without water, clouds that are
carried with a tempest . . . For when they speak great
swelling words of vanity, they allure through the lusts of
the flesh, through much wantonness, those that were clean
escaped from them who live in error." (2 Peter 2:17, 18)
This shows they have influence over others until they allure
them away from the true path. They promise them liberty
and tell them it is wrong to recognize government and that
the Holy Ghost should lead them and no one should have
the oversight or pre-eminence over another. And "While
they promise them liberty, they themselves are the servants
of corruption." (2 Peter 2:19)

You will please notice that when Balaam had tried in vain
to curse Israel twice that in the third attempt he instructed
Balak to build the seven altars and offer the seven bullocks
and seven rams, but "When Balaam saw that it please the
Lord to bless Israel, he went not, as at other times, to seek
for enchantments," but pronounced a blessing on them and
acknowledged they were God's peculiar people.

When Philip went down to Samaria and preached Christ
unto them, Simon, the sorcerer, believed, and fell right in
with Philip and acknowledged that he was a man of God.
This man went so far as to be baptized by Philip, thereby lending his influence in favor of God's work and people. But when Peter and John went down there they discovered that his heart was not right in the sight of God.
Before this he had been looked upon by all as "the great
power of God." Although his heart was not right, he could
point out God's people. Balaam's heart was not right, but
he could point out God's people.

See another instance, Acts 16:16: "And it came to pass,
as we went to prayer, a certain damsel possessed with a spirit of divination met us, which brought her masters much
gain by soothsaying. The same followed Paul and us, and

cried, saying, These men are the servants of the most high God, which shew unto us the way of salvation." This woman was both a soothsayer and a diviner, like Balaam, and she could point out those men of God and seemed to take a delight in following with them and saying they were men of God until Paul became grieved and commanded the spirit to come out of her. "And he came out the same hour."

For fear some may misunderstand our meaning and think we are objecting to divine guidance, or being led by the Spirit, because of some expressions in this article, I wish to state that I am in full harmony with divine guidance, and those who know me well know I teach that the Holy Ghost is our guide and His promptings and leadings should be obeyed. I am only showing how the Balaam doctrine will cause people to so nearly imitate the genuine in their expressions and actions that it can scarcely be detected. Some have expressed it as their opinion that Balaam was a good man and a real prophet of God because the record shows how he consulted with God in everything before he acted, and it has been only with difficulty that we have convinced them that he was a bad man, a deceiver and false prophet. Those who believe Balaam was good because he recognized God in his dealings with Balak would be an easy prey to those in possession and under the influence of the Balaam doctrine today.

I could name a number of people who have evidently been under this influence. Their fruits have shown it plainly. Some have been right among us and to all appearance the best and most spiritual people in the services. Some of these have confessed to me that, "the Lord showed them" to do certain things that the Bible condemns.

This is another proof of our need of the gifts of the Spirit—wisdom, discernment, etc., that we may be better equipped for the war that is raging at this present time. Beloved, we must move up and meet the conditions, and receive the gifts, or meet with disappointment and defeat.

ZIMRI'S ADDRESS

In continuing this subject I wish to call attention to the address delivered by Zimri to Moses and the congregation in defiance of government and the God-given laws to Israel, while he was under the influence of the damnable Balaam doctrine just before his death. I give it in full as recorded by Josephus, the Jewish historian:

"But Zimri arose up . . . and said, 'Yes, indeed Moses, thou art at liberty to make use of such laws as thou art so fond of, and hast, by accustoming thyself to them made them firm; otherwise, if things had not been thus, thou hadst often been punished before now, and hadst known that the Hebrews are not easily put upon; but thou shalt not have me one of thy followers in thy tyrannical commands, for thou dost nothing else hitherto, but under pretense of laws, and of God, wickedly impose on us slavery, and gain dominion to thyself, while thou deprivest us of the sweetness of life, which consists in acting according to our own wills, and is the right of free men, and of those that have no lord over them. Nay, indeed, this man Moses is harder upon the Hebrews than were the Egyptians themselves as pretending to punish, according to his laws, everyone's acting what is most disagreeable to himself; but thou thyself better deservest to suffer punishment, who presumest to abolish what everyone acknowledges to be good for him, and aimest to make thy single opinion to have more force than that of all the rest: and what I now do, and think to be right, I shall not hereafter deny to be according to my own sentiments. I have married, as thou sayest rightly, a strange woman, and thou hearest what I do from myself as from one that is free; for truly I did not intend to conceal myself. I also own that I sacrificed to those gods to whom you do not think it fit to sacrifice, and I think it right to come at truth by inquiring of many people, not liking to live under tyranny, to suffer the whole hope of my life to depend upon one man; nor shall any one find cause to rejoice who declares himself to have more authority over my actions than myself.' "

Surely the readers will see in this speech a masterpiece of boldness and contemptuous disregard to government. This is none other than anarchy. This man was one of the princes of Israel, the head of the tribe of Simeon—one who would be expected to be loyal to his government for the sake of his high position if for nothing else. In this speech he reproached his own fathers, the man Moses whom God had chosen to govern Israel and execute His laws, and the God of his fathers and His laws, and scornfully and disdainfully declared himself an anarchist. This prince of Israel never would have been guilty of this baneful disregard for government and his God, had he not been overpowered by the accursed Balaam doctrine.

I wish to call attention to the close resemblance of this man's speech and the eighth verse of Jude. "Likewise also these filthy dreamers defile the flesh, despise dominion, and speak evil of dignities."

Jude informs us that at the very time when God's people should earnestly contend for the faith once delivered unto the saints "there are certain men crept in unawares," and these are the same people he calls filthy dreamers that defile the flesh, despise dominion, and speak evil of dignities (just like Zimri did), and proceeds to show in the eleventh verse that "they have gone in the way of Cain, and ran greedily after the error of Balaam." This shows that the Balaam doctrine will prevail in a measure and come right in amongst God's people who are earnestly contending for the faith. If contending for the faith refers to us at this time, then we may expect that the Balaam doctrine will be exerting its baneful influence in our midst. In verse twelve, Jude further states that those holding to the Balaam doctrine will be spots in the feasts of charity that God's people are enjoying, and that they will take part in the service just like they were God's children and enjoy it as they feed themselves without fear.

If one who is acting for God in some high position is accused of trying to gain dominion over others, though he is only doing his duty; and such accusers declare they do not expect to have a "boss" over them and reject God's order and organization, they can well be classed with those influenced by the Balaam doctrine. Jude says such "separate themselves, sensual, having not the Spirit." (Jude 19)

Many of those we call our own people are taking up the theory of Zimri, which was inspired by the Balaam doctrine, and are going to hear some of the many different teachings that are making the rounds. They say they like to hear all sides and learn what others teach. This certainly shows rather an unsettled and dissatisfied condition, and that they are not content with God's laws and government.

The Balaam doctrine allured Zimri and got him so fastened in its coil until he was unable to throw it off so it led him to his death. Peter and Jude both declare that those who follow Balaam's doctrine will be led to their own destruction. "But these, as natural brute beasts . . . speak evil of the things that they understand not; and shall utterly perish in their own corruption." (2 Peter 2:12) "Woe unto them! for they have gone in the way of Cain, and ran greedily after the error of Balaam for reward, and perish in the gainsaying of Core." (Jude 11)

LAST DAYS

In the glowing light that God's Word throws upon the Balaam doctrine, the close resemblance it has to the real truth and the fascinating effect it has upon its adherents, I tremble for the future of some people I know. Some came to us a few years ago and claimed the Lord showed them that we were right and wanted to enlist with us in the battle. They took the obligation and were enthusiastic and worked earnestly for awhile, but later claimed they changed their views and did not believe this was the true Church of God and separated themselves from us. Doesn't this look about like the effect the Balaam doctrine had upon Zimri? John tells us: "Whereby we know that it is the last time. They went out from us, but they were not of us; for if they had been of us, they would no doubt have continued with us: but they went out, that they might be made manifest that they were not all of us." (1 John 2:18, 19)

While some, like Zimri, have evidently been caught in the fascinating coils of the doctrine of Balaam and joined the anarchists and "do as I please" and "according to my own will" solitude, others are seeing the glorious light of the Church of God, and scores and hundreds are casting away their preconceived notions and traditions and opinions and self-wills and coming "to their own company" (Acts 4:23) amid songs and triumphant shouts of victory with everlasting joy upon their heads and obtaining joy and gladness. (Isa. 51:11)

Second Coming and
the Resurrection

That He (the Lord) is going to return to earth is an absolute fact according to Scripture. And we know there is much to be done to make ready, but I must insist that the exercise of governmental authority and obedience thereto must not be ignored or thrust aside. Those who despise government will not be in the Church that the Lord presents to Himself.

There is a difference in the coming of the Lord to resurrect the dead saints and to rapture away the Church, and the coming of Christ with His saints to reign on the earth. Here is where some get confused. But such confusion must be perfectly cleared up among our people.

At His first appearing He does not come to the earth—He comes close enough to call the saints—that is, the dead saints and the Church—to meet Him in the air, and they soar away to the marriage supper, where they will remain, perhaps, for three years and a half, while the tribulations are bursting forth upon the earth. Then at the proper time, Jesus and His army will mount the white horses, and ride down from heaven and capture and bind the devil and cast him into the bottomless pit where he shall remain for a thousand years.

That the dead will come forth when the Lord calls is confirmed by words that fell from the lips of Him who spake as never man spake: "Marvel not at this: for the hour is coming, in the which all that are in the graves shall hear his voice, And shall come forth; they that have done good, unto the resurrection of life; and they that have done evil, unto the resurrection of damnation." (John 5:28, 29) The above Scripture seems to indicate that the saints and the wicked will be resurrected at the same time, but the Bible plainly states that the wicked will not be resurrected for a thousand years after the righteous come forth: "But the rest of the dead (wicked) lived not again until the thousand years were finished. This is the first resurrection. Blessed and holy is he that hath part in the first resurrection: on such the second death hath no power, but they shall be priests of God and of Christ, and shall reign with him a thousand years." (Revelation 20:5, 6)

The resurrection is the hope of the Christian. Studying about it sometimes, I can hardly wait for it.

And the Angel said He is coming again. Truly the resurrection and glory awaiting the saints is looked for with joyful anticipation, and there are many anxious for the time to come. We expect His coming to exceed His ascension in glory and thrills. There is no question about the shout and trumpet sound at that time, and it is unnecessary to draw on our imagination for material to describe it, fo rthe writers of the sacred Book furnished sufficient material and of the very best to tell the story.

When we get all the Scriptures classified we read the conclusion plain and clear. At the appointed time, He will descend with a shout and the sound of a trumpet and call from their graves the saints of all ages who have fallen asleep in faith. And soon after the dead shall have risen, and come forth singing, the living saints who measure up to the full requirements will be changed in a moment into the glorified state. Then, at the appointed time, they will be caught up to meet the Lord in the air. I will not attempt a description of this meeting, but I am sure it will be an all-glorious affair.

Not all of this glorious company will be the Bride, but all will have the high honor of partaking of the supper. The length of time to be occupied in the marriage ceremony and the ceremonial feast is unknown, but whether it will be three years and a half, as some believe, or seven years or forty years, not one of those present will become wearied or lose interest. Doubtless the thrilling interest will increase hour by hour. The very best entertainment heaven can afford will be given the guests, and special heavenly honors will be heaped upon the Bridegroom and the beautiful bride.

This will be a gorgeous and magnificent affair . . . and to miss it by disobedience or failing God one hairbreadth will be enough to cause regrets to haunt one a million years. And this is a reason for my carefulness in obedience and close Christian living.

When this gigantic spread is all finished, and full preparations have been made, organization completed, so every one will know his place and position, the march to earth will commence. The white horses will be mounted, Jesus will head the glorious cavalcade, banners will be floating, heavenly music will be rendered on the way—doubtless, angels will watch this grand descent with amazement and wonder. On, on, will ride the white army until the armies of earth will catch a glimpse of the approaching host, when they will begin to defy their onward march. But all their efforts will be in vain. This army will arrive! Jesus' feet will touch Olivet from whence He ascended, and immediately we will take possession of the whole earth to reign triumphant a thousand years!

"With this blessed hope before us,

Let no harp remain unstrung,

Let the mighty heavenly chorus,

Onward roll from tongue to tongue:

Christ is coming!

Come, Thou blessed Prince of Peace!"

Move Up A Little Every Day

Keep Up A Brave Fight For Experimental Religion Taught By The Bible

GRACE PROVIDES THRILLING ADVENTURES

There is no place to stop or slow down. The world is on the whirl and the Christian religion should be more so, but not in the same way. The world has its advocates of fashion and sociology as well as trades, business and politics. They are straining every nerve to make advancement in their particular field of service. Their objective is to move up a little every day and take on new force and prepare new attractions. In this they boast of their success. They are lauded by their admirers for their inventions and display of wisdom. Every leading advocate of his particular line of work has his throng of admirers who stand behind him with their means, hand-claps of encouragement, and they step right up and hold the ground their favorite leader has taken while he goes on with his work in discovering new fields yet unknown.

It is not our purpose to follow the example of the world and to introduce worldly plans and practices into our religion, but it may be well to give a statement made by Jesus as an incentive to us to move up a little every day and to show how we may profit by some things we may see in the world. "The children of this world are in their generation wiser than the children of light," He said. (Luke 16:8) He does not say it should be that way, but He states it as an actual existing fact. We may never be able to overcome this condition and change it so the Lord can speak otherwise of us in the last days, but at any rate we should heed His command and be as wise as serpents and as harmless as doves. (Matt. 10:16) And acting wisely in this respect will surely cause us to move up in our experience a little every day.

One that is only converted should earnestly seek to make some forward move in his new found field of life. To do this was a special objective in my life before I knew sanctification. I believed it should be in others, but now that sanctification is so well known among our people I do not advise one to remain in that state long enough to follow my own early experience. I rather advise a convert to whip right through to the experience of sanctification before he has time to make much of a move forward, more than to move forward into the deeper experience. And when he undertakes it those interested should cheer him on by their prayers and songs until he finds himself completely relieved of the tantalizing presence of the Ishmael nature.

And then when one is sanctified is the best time for him to press right on through to the heights of the baptism of the Holy Ghost and fire. But to those who are sanctified and have not yet had the pleasure of the infilling experience, the advice is given by Paul and others to keep on moving up a little every day toward the higher heights of the higher and fuller experience. And even when one is filled with the Holy Ghost there are other attainments to strive for so there is no place to stop or slow down. This statement and advice is verified by Paul when he says, "Forgetting those things which are behind, and reaching forth unto those things which are before, I press toward the mark for the prize of the high calling of God in Christ Jesus." And to further prove that there is no stopping place I quote Paul again where he says, "Whereto we have already attained, let us walk by the same rule, let us mind the same thing." (Phil. 3:13-16) No matter where we are in our experience we are to burn the bridges behind us and move on to higher attainments. And there will always be the prize before us until the sound of the trumpet is heard which will call us to the life of glorification so that we will not be marked when Jesus makes His long looked for appearance. But how can people hope to be found clothed who have had a touch of the experimental religion?

Seeing that experimental religion is becoming so unpopular even among some of the same classes which formerly enjoyed it, how necessary it is for us who know it to keep up a brave fight for the Bible kind of experimental religion. The world does not know it and the advocates of the popular religion of our day do not and cannot tell them about it. The masses are to be pitied. There are multitudes that would accept the true way if they could only hear the Word enough to generate faith in the Christ who gives the experience. Honest, sincere souls want an experience that produces feeling to which they receive the witness of the Spirit (Rom. 8:16) to show that they are children of God and saved from their sins. (Matt. 1:21) And this calls for more faithful service on the part of those who know the truth and have the experience.

I cannot understand what people can hope for at death when they have only formally accepted Christ by giving the minister their hand and joining some church when Jesus explained to Nicodemus so clearly that "Except a man be born again, he cannot see the kingdom of God." (John 3:3) This was a puzzle to Nicodemus, and it must be such a puzzle to the popular religionists of our day that they do not want the humility of becoming as a little child again with their erudition and trained intellects. It seems they would rather lose their souls than to submit to Matthew 18:3— "Except ye be converted, and become as little children, ye shall not enter into the kingdom of heaven." Knowing conditions as we do we think it is no wonder that Jude instructed us, yea, gave us orders to "earnestly contend for for the faith which was once delivered unto the saints." The opposers of experimental religion are determined to exterminate it from the roll of religion and it will be totally annihilated if somebody does not fight to retain it and lift up the same standard of former years. I consider this a part of our duty in this great revolution. Somebody is trying to hold it up and keep it in its place. And the command of God comes to us through the prophet Isaiah saying, "Go through, go through the gates; prepare ye the way of the people; cast up, cast up the highway; gather out the stones; lift up a standard for the people." (Isa. 62:10) Gates are bars or solid obstacles to stop the passage through what would otherwise be an aperture or opening. Isaiah's statement would infer that we are to be barred out of some places, but he tells us to go through these obstructions and hindrances and lift up a standard to the people who are behind these gates. And Jesus Himself declares that even the gates of hell shall not prevail against His Church, and her standard of teaching shall go right through these gates that are intended to keep them away from the people on the other side of these obstructions.

Isaiah says to go through the gates, and Jesus says the gates shall not hold us out and even the gates of hell shall not prevail against His Church. With all this kind of encouragement where is the time to retreat or back down? Therefore it is our duty to keep up a brave fight for experimental religion taught by the Bible, and God will give us grace for thrilling adventures. The opposition is strong and becoming stronger every day, but we hear Isaiah again as he shouts out the command of the Lord, "Awake, awake, put on strength, O arm of the LORD; awake, as in the ancient days, in the generations of old. Art thou not it that hath cut Rahab, and wounded the dragon? Art thou not it which hath dried the sea, the waters of the great deep; that hath made the depths of the sea a way for the ransomed to pass over?" (Isa. 51:9, 10) Does this not show how the gates were closed against the Lord's people; and yet not even the sea or the river could prevent them from going through? God said, Go through, and they went. A thrilling adventure, but these gates could not prevail against their passage.

I do not know what kind of thrilling adventures we will be called upon to make in order to get the message of life to the people beyond the gates, but God says to go through the gates, and Jesus says the gates shall not prevail against His Church, which shows that every barrier shall be broken down as we move forward under the mighty power of the Holy Ghost. Even the gates of opposition will be cast aside so the word of life can reach the people. This looks like a strong statement to make, but I feel that God's Word is back of it and that makes me feel that I am on safe footing. Many places and people are closed against us now, but not any more so than was the Red Sea closed against Israel under the leadership of Moses, and when God told Moses to go forward He made the gate open and let His host pass through. That gate of the Red Sea could not prevail against that mighty host when God said, Go forward. And when God says to His Church to go forward the gates of hell cannot prevent or prevail against it. Hallelujah! And now my soul leaps and dances as I read from Isaiah again: "Therefore the redeemed of the Lord shall return, and come with singing unto Zion; and everlasting joy shall be upon their head; they shall obtain gladness and joy; and sorrow and mourning shall flee away." (Isa. 51:11)

There was the Jordan river overflowing its banks as a barrier or gate to prevent the entrance of Israel into the promised land, but God said, Go forward, and Joshua repeated the command and started the priests right into the water which at first refused to give way, but down came the battering ram of faith that broke the power of that gate and the water was forced to give way for the passage of that mighty host. Sometimes the gates we are to go through may become sullen and stubborn and refuse to open and get out of the way so His Church can pass through, but persistent faith and thrilling adventure will break the power of opposition so she can march through with her banners waving and the standard floating in the beautiful breeze at the top of the mast. No, not even the gates of hell shall prevail against the passage of the Lord's Church into the promises God has made to her. The oppositions at times will become stubborn and only reluctantly give way, but a constant pressure will force an opening.

There was the wall around Jericho. Israel must get inside the city, but there stood the stone wall guarding against the entry at every place. Orders were given to commence the march around. Orders must be obeyed. They were God's orders and Joshua enforced them. It required some delay and the exercise of much patience, but when the final charge was made and every man went shouting right straight toward the city the walls fell down flat and could not prevail against God's host any longer. Israel was barred out. The gates were strong, but at a given time Israel marched in. Listen! The gates of hell shall not prevail against—cannot prevent His Church rising and shining and performing its mission in the earth. We only have to be faithful and very courageous and down will go the gates or they will be blown up with mighty explosives of God's power.

"For whatsoever things were written aforetime were written for our learning, that we through patience and comfort of the scriptures might have hope" (Rom. 15:4), to see the Church—the true standard, rise to its proper height according to prophecy. There may be many thrilling adventures, but the Scriptures must be fulfilled. God only wants faithful men and women who will obey His instructions and the results will follow according to His will, and we will surely move up a little every day. Hallelujah!

The Ministers

God's Messengers Are Commissioned To Feed
The Church of God

A few moments ago I said, "I think we have the best set of ministers that this world can produce." I have not changed my mind, but it may be well for me to add that although they are so good and great and powerful there may be some room for improvement. I hope the time will soon come when all the ministers will become so engrossed and absorbed with their work as ministers that they will put all their energies into this special work and let others attend to other business not pertaining directly to the Church and her special interests. I am afraid too many of our ministers have their minds too much divided to render the very best service to God and His Church. I offer no criticism for what has been done the past year in the way of engaging in business and seeking employment to earn a livelihood, but this has been a hard year—an off year—and I hope this condition will not continue. We are in need of a larger number of ministers who have no business occupation whatever—those who have nothing else to do but preach, pray, and attend to their ministerial duties. May we have them the coming year? Surely the next year will bring about more prosperous conditions in the country so the ministers will be better provided for and will not be compelled to seek other employment for a livelihood.

Special effort should be made by all the ministers to improve in their knowledge of the Bible and their preaching. This can be done by acting upon Paul's advice where he says, "Study to shew thyself approved unto God, a workman that needeth not to be ashamed, rightly dividing the word of truth." There is not time for vacant staring or idle moments. Every moment is of too much value to allow it to pass without being used. If you have to wait a few minutes for some reason, snatch up the Bible, or a book, or a paper, and get a few thoughts to store away for future use. Improve your mind. Make it work. Don't let it scatter about and catch on to a lot of things that are degrading instead of elevating. Always strive to make gains. Don't just depend on preaching a few sermons that you have been over so many times that you almost have them memorized. Enlarge your field. Get up new subjects in a new way. Aspire to higher things and better methods. Don't give up and lay down because you feel bad. Spur yourself up, study over your lessons so hard that it will make your head hurt. Then you are improving Don't let your mind drift about like a child. Put away childish things and be a man.

In your preaching never let a spirit get hold of you that will make you preach rough and harsh. Always be mellow and present the truth in a way to edify instead of stupify. This rough, harsh, scolding, gouging, bemeaning, accusing, beating and banging kind of preaching is out of date. The minister that hangs to that kind will soon be out of a job. Tell the truth, preach the gospel, do not shun to declare the whole counsel of God, but learn to do it in a way that will be effective for good, and have a drawing effect instead of a driving effect. This singling out someone to preach at and accuse him in public and claim God has revealed his "black heart and hideous crimes," when nine times out of ten or more the sermon has been inspired by some tale teller who has told the preacher some reports on the man instead of God being in it at all, will have to stop. There is a strong sentiment against such, and the preacher that does this will not be wanted the next year. I have heard of a few good pastors who have lovingly and deliberately stopped a few of those rough, bemeaning, accusing and abusing kind of evangelists, and would not allow them to preach in their pulpits. I hope we will never have any of this kind to give us trouble in the Church of God, or if there may have been some surely they will not do that way again. I know of some who have been on that line who are as placid as a little lamb today.

Never allow yourself to be discouraged or take a spell of the blues. Always look on the bright side of things. If someone tells you a doleful tale about a brother or sister or church, try to think it may not be as serious as represented. Remember that some people have a tendency toward looking on the dark side of things, and you must not be influenced by them. I very frequently receive a report from two persons about the condition of the same church. One describes it as being in a prosperous condition and everything moving on nicely, while the other describes it as being almost gone —some of the members moved away, some backslidden, others do not attend, the pastor neglecting his duty, etc., etc. Both are sincere, both are honest, and each gives the information as he sees it, but one is looking on the dark side with a pair of discouraged eyes, while the other has the victory and feels like everybody else has it too. A minister is supposed to have the victory all the time and if he is about to get faint hearted he should brace up and sing.

We'll never be discouraged,
  Though difficulties rise

And seem to stop the pathway
  That leadeth to the skies,

We'll ever travel onward,
  Not fearing any foe,

And ever looking upward
  As marching on we go.

The Enormous Price
Paid for the Church

Our Christ Must Have Considered It Extremely Valuable to Purchase It At Such a Cost

WE SHOULD DEMONSTRATE OUR VALUE

O, if I could only do justice to this subject! To do this will require something more than mere brains and intellect. I will have to draw upon the resources of heaven coupled with special revelations and inspiration. The Book God has given us will have to be called into use. The Holy Spirit who is our constant dependence will be depended upon to bring into use information both new and old. We ourselves may need to be expanded in order to comprehend that which is too wonderful for the natural. To only get a little glimpse into the unsearchable riches of God's plans and glory for His Church gives cause for sensational thrills to chase one another up and down one's soul.

The subject may be incomprehensible to the natural mind, but I feel it is time for the members of the Church of God to begin to realize, to an extent at least, the high value placed upon it by one that knows the true value of things far better than any of the most capable experts of earth who are chosen to judge values. I have been trying to creep upon the edge of this subject at intervals for a long time, and this is about all I hope to do now in this message. But I am becoming so anxious for our people to begin to realize the high value of the purchased possession that I feel I must make some mention of it occasionally.

The most of us know what the Bible says about the enormous price paid for the Church, but without some comparison more fitted for us to understand we are apt to fall far below the real value in our estimations. And I want us to begin to understand more fully "who we are" so we will not continue too long to underestimate our value. I want us to more fully feel our importance and thus live a life of high value—clean, bright and glistening. This is to be to the praise of the glory of His grace, and to make ourselves more attractive so others will be drawn this way. My desire is more fully portrayed in the words of the great apostle Paul who says:

"According as he hath chosen us in him before the foundation of the world, that we should be holy and without blame before him in love: Having predestinated us unto the adoption of children by Jesus Christ to himself, according to the good pleasure of his will, To the praise of the glory of his grace, wherein he hath made us accepted in the beloved. In whom we have redemption through his blood, the forgiveness of sins, according to the riches of his grace; Wherein he hath abounded toward us in all wisdom and prudence; Having made known unto us the mystery of his will, according to his good pleasure which he hath purposed in himself: That in the dispensation of the fulness of times he might gather together in one all things in Christ, both which are in heaven, and which are on earth; even in him: In whom also we have obtained an inheritance, being predestinated according to the purpose of him who worketh all things after the counsel of his own will: That we should be to the praise of his glory, who first trusted in Christ." (Eph. 1:4-12)

Personal representatives of another should endeavor to measure up to the same type and standard of the person represented. We could not think of a low grade person properly representing one of a high grade. And to be to the praise of the person represented, one would of necessity have to talk, act and live in a manner that would perfectly satisfy and honor the person represented. An uneducated person could not be a good representative of one of high attainments in education. Neither could a highly educated person be the proper kind of a personal representative of one who is uneducated. A disagreeable, profane, disreputable, profligate, depraved, corrupt son could not be an honor to a father and mother in high standing with fine moral principles and possessing good Christian qualities. Such a son could not be a good personal representative of his parents. If the people were to judge the parents by such a defiled and foul-mouth son they would be brought into ill repute and disgrace.

Jesus came to this world as a personal representative of His Father. Knowing His Father as He did and being to the praise of His glory He could well represent His Father. And that He knew well enough to be His very best representative is voiced by the following words given by Jesus Himself:

"All things are delivered unto me of my Father: and no man knoweth the Son, but the Father; neither knoweth any man the Father, save the Son, and he to whomsoever the Son will reveal him." (Matt. 11:27)

To carry this analogy on a little further to assist in illustrating the truth I am trying to get to my audience, I wish to add a statement given by the great apostle Paul. Read it and understand.

"Let this mind be in you, which was also in Christ Jesus: Who, being in the form of God, thought it not robbery to be equal with God: But made himself of no reputation, and took upon him the form of a servant, and was made in the likeness of men: And being found in fashion as a man, he humbled himself, and became obedient unto death, even the death of the cross." (Phil. 2:5-8)

But while Jesus, who was God's personal representative in this world, and for that reason did not consider it robbery to be equal with Him, and made Himself of no reputation by becoming a servant, yet He did no sin, neither did He anything that would bring disgrace or ill repute upon His Father. This is voiced by Peter who wrote thus of Him:

"Who did no sin, neither was guile found in his mouth: Who, when he was reviled, reviled not again; when he suffered, he threatened not; but committed himself to him that judgeth righteously." (1 Peter 2:22, 23)

Now, after having dwelt upon the importance of being and living "to the praise of the glory of His grace" which is the same as living in such a way that we can have Christ's approval upon us, I now wish to further consider the enormous price paid for the Church. This may be shown to an extent by referring to the multitudes of sacrifices made on altars as a type of the one sacrifice made by Himself to purchase the Church. And truly all the sacrifices that were ever slain, and inestimable in money value, are only a small value to compare with the one that purchased the Church. And before going further into the subject please read:

"Take heed therefore unto yourselves, and to all the flock, over the which the Holy Ghost hath made you overseers, to feed the church of God, which he hath purchased with his own blood." (Acts 20:28)

Sacrifices pointing to this special blood sacrifice have been made and offered all along since the first one of which we have an account, made soon after the creation of Adam and Eve. This seems to have been a voluntary offering by the second son of our first parents. But it was a beginning, and served its purpose in pointing out the purchase price of the Church of God. Read about it:

"And Abel, he also brought of the firstlings of his flock and of the fat thereof. And the Lord had respect unto Abel and to his offering." (Gen. 4:4)

The Bible is silent as to the money value of this first offering, but it must have been quite valuable. It was worth enough so God gave His attention to it and respected it as the beginning of blood sacrifices to point out the enormous value of the Church of God which was later to be purchased by the blood of the Son of God.

The second blood sacrifice of which we have any definite knowledge as given in the Bible is the one offered by Noah just after the flood. It will be well to give attention to this one because it had its part in the drama, also. Now read a short sketch about Noah's sacrifice as you keep in mind the purchase price of the Church. It is evident that the sacrifice made by Noah had a larger money value than that offered by Abel. This also has a special signigcation pointing to the one great sacrifice of the Son of God Himself. Read:

"And Noah builded an altar unto the LORD; and took of
every clean beast, and of every clean fowl, and offered burnt
offerings on the altar." (Gen. 8:20)

I wish also to call attention to the third blood sacrifice
which was made by Abram who later became Abraham and
pronounced the father of the faithful. This third one carries with it special prominence and signification, comparing
well with our third experience which is named "baptize you
with the Holy Ghost and with fire," according to Matthew
3:11. And our record gives the kinds of animals and fowls
used in this special blood sacrifice. Read some of the story:

"And he said unto him, Take me an heifer of three years
old, and a she goat of three years old, and a ram of three
years old, and a turtledove, and a young pigeon. And he
took unto him all these, and divided them in the midst, and
laid each piece one against another: but the birds divided
he not. And when the fowls came down upon the carcasses,
Abram drove them away. And when the sun was going
down, a deep sleep fell upon Abram; and lo, an horror of
great darkness fell upon him. And he said unto Abram,
Know of a surety that thy seed shall be a stranger in a land
that is not theirs, and shall serve them; and they shall af-
flict them four hundred years; And also that nation, whom
they shall serve, will I judge: and afterward shall they
come out with great substance. And thou shalt go to thy
fathers in peace; thou shalt be buried in a good old age.
But in the fourth generation they shall come hither again:
for the iniquity of the Amorites is not yet full. And it came
to pass, that, when the sun went down, and it was dark, behold a smoking furnace, and a burning lamp that passed
between those pieces." (Gen. 15:9-17)

During this sacrificial ceremony darkness came upon
Abram that compares well with the darkness that over-
shadowed the cross when the purchase price was being paid
for the Church. Here also God announced the sojourn of four
hundred years in Egypt, which program called for Joseph
to be carried into Egypt and sold as a slave, and everything
else contained in the story. For this sacrifice the fire was
furnished in a miraculous manner like the one offered by

Elijah on Mount Carmel. This was a wonderful demonstration of the presence and power of God and marks a special epoch in the life of Abram as well as in the story that continues unbroken until the final enormous price was paid over for the Church.

The next and fourth sacrifice to be considered is that of Abraham offering his own son Isaac. This was indeed such a sacrifice upon which no value could be placed, however, a little later a ram was substituted. But Abraham went on in good faith and proved his obedience and faith. Isaac was a special type of Jesus, and of this incident it is said:

"By faith Abraham, when he was tried, offered up Isaac: and he that had received the promises offered up his only begotton son, Of whom it was said, That in Isaac shall thy seed be called: Accounting that God was able to raise him up, even from the dead; from whence also he received him in a figure." (Heb. 11:17-19)

After this, innumerable sacrifices were made unto the Lord. When the law was given on Mount Sinai the sacrificial offerings were incorporated therein. From that time until the day Jesus cried with a loud voice and gave up the Ghost countless millions of beasts and fowls were slain and offered as sacrifices unto God all for the purpose of pointing to the Lamb of God who purchased the Church with His own blood. Besides all the people being required to offer sacrifices once a year, special sacrifices were required on special occasions. And besides these, special people offered multitudes of animals and fowls on special occasions. Among the number of those who made large offerings were David and Solomon. A few verses here will assist in telling the story for the purpose of swelling the countless millions of costly sacrifices, so our minds can better comprehend the whole story of all the sacrifices, every one of which pointed to the purchase price of the Church. Read:

"And they brought in the ark of the Lord, and set it in his place, in the midst of the tabernacle that David had pitched for it: and David offered burnt offerings and peace offerings before the LORD. (2 Sam. 6:17)

"And the king, and all Israel with him, offered sacrifice before the LORD. And Solomon offered a sacrifice of peace offerings, which he offered unto the LORD, two and twenty thousand oxen, and an hundred and twenty thousand sheep. So the king and all the children of Israel dedicated the house of the LORD." (1 Kings 8:62, 63)

All of these at one time besides the countless thousands of red heifers, oxen, sheep, goats, fowls, lambs and whatever else may have been included in the multitudes of sacrifices that were made by the millions of people year after year for many centuries. The shed blood from these sacrifices would have made broad and deep rivers. And every drop of blood, the broad rivers, the lowing of the herds as they were driven to the altars, and the bleating of the sheep, helped to tell the wonderful story of the purchase price of the Church of which we now have the honor of being members. Put a value upon all of the animals and fowls that were ever offered at the market price and no mind can comprehend the countless millions and billions of dollars as a price paid for them. And then to all of this vast sum add all of the gold and silver and precious stones discovered and still hidden and then add other decillions of money values and still all of this magnitudinous amount of wealth would not equal the price of the precious blood of the Son of God that purchased the Church of God. After all of this incomprehensible comparison then there can remain no wonder why He calls it His Church—"My Church," He said. The wonder comes in the inestimable value He has placed upon the value of the souls and bodies of the members of the Church He has purchased.

After having given attention to the story as told, surely no one can question but that an enormous price was paid for the Church. Then with this fact before us, and knowing the judgment of God with respect to values, we are bound to admit that we are a valuable set. Our Christ must have considered it—the Church, extremely valuable to purchase it at such a cost. Our Lord Jesus Christ must have regarded it as worth all it cost or He would not have paid the high price for it. Then since we—the members—are considered of such extreme worth we should demonstrate our value and not try to belittle ourselves. Instead of this we should keep ourselves polished and shining and glistening like the diamonds all the time. A statement of Paul is worthy of inserting here as further proof and for the purpose of aiding us in better understanding the whole mystery that is hid from the world and will never be revealed of them except by and through the Church of God, its members and ministers. Please give close attention as you read.

"That the God of our Lord Jesus Christ, the Father of glory, may give unto you the spirit of wisdom and revelation in the knowledge of him: The eyes of your understanding being enlightened; that ye may know what is the hope of his calling, and what the riches of the glory of his inheritance in the saints, And what is the exceeding greatness of his power to usward who believe, according to the working of his mighty power, Which he wrought in Christ, when he raised him from the dead, and set him at his own right hand in the heavenly places, Far above all principality, and power, and might, and dominion, and every name that is named, not only in this world, but also in that which is to come: And hath put all things under his feet, and gave him to be the head over all things to the church, Which is his body, the fulness of him that filleth all in all." (Eph. 1:17-23)

Since we are of such great value to Him who has purchased us, then we are supposed to serve Him to the full value of the purchase price. And this will automatically require a demonstration of our value. And this cannot be done by our weakening down and admitting that we are sold for more than we are worth. Jesus has purchased us at the great cost described above, then who of us wants to admit that he has been purchased at a higher price than he is worth? And we surely do not consider that He has purchased us at such a high price simply to take us to heaven to sit down and rest and never perform any service. Such a view as that seems out of place to me in the light of the Holy Scriptures. Since we are to fill all in all, then there is some expanding to do. And since we are to grow up into Him in all things and be like Him in order to perform and serve well, there may be some changes to be made in us to enable us to really demonstrate our worth to Him. Thus Paul speaks further and says:

"But we all, with open fact beholding as in a glass the glory of the LORD, are changed into the same image from glory to glory, even as by the Spirit of the Lord. Therefore seeing we have this ministry, as we have received mercy, we faint not; But have renounced the hidden things of dishonesty, not walking in craftiness, nor handling the word of God deceitfully; but by manifestation of the truth commending our selves to every man's conscience in the sight of God." (2 Cor. 3:18; 4:1, 2)

I am trying to impress on the minds of my audience that we should prove ourselves worth the high price paid for us. Otherwise why would we not be fakes or like shoddy goods or dishonest? If a man receives high wages than he makes himself worth to his employer, what is he? And since the Church has been purchased at such a high cost it is our duty as members to brace up and demonstrate our worth by service instead of becoming faint and weak. Instead of being dishonest toward our Master who has paid such a high price for us we should render unto Him honest and faithful service. And I am not yet convinced that the only service we are to give Him is limited to this world. But this is our place of service now and we should "walk worthy of the Lord unto all pleasing, being fruitful in every good work, and increasing in the knowledge of him."

Thou Shalt Not
Commit Adultery

Beware of the Lust of the Flesh

HAVE CHRISTIAN FELLOWSHIP, BUT AVOID
UNDUE INTIMACY

"Hast thou not known? hast thou not heard, that the ever-lasting God, the LORD, the Creator of the ends of the earth, fainteth not, neither is weary . . . He giveth power to the faint; and to them that have no might he increaseth strength. Even the youths shall faint and be weary, and the young men shall utterly fall: But they that wait upon the Lord shall renew their strength; they shall mount up with wings as eagles; they shall run, and not be weary; and they shall walk, and not faint." (Isa. 40:28-31)

"Fear thou not; for I am with thee: be not dismayed; for I am thy God: I will strengthen thee; yea, I will help thee; yea, I will uphold thee with the right hand of my righteous-ness . . . No weapon that is formed against thee shall prosper; and every tongue that shall rise against thee in judgment thou shalt condemn." (Isa. 31:10; 54:17)

These are God's promises to the grand old Church of God. Who would not want to be a member? How many are glad you are members now? Yes, I am glad I am a member. You are glad you are members. Our joy over this one thing abides and abounds. But our beloved—the Church—has been made to hang her head with shame because of unwise actions of some of her sons and daughters. They have brought reproach and disgrace upon her fair head. This is sad indeed, but I feel pressed in my spirit to mention this here and now as a warn-ing for the future.

But what is it that is so dreadful? What has occurred that has caused such a reference here? Would to God it was unnecessary to present a theme that is so obnoxious. The fact of it is, that, both men and women who have once been shining lights in the Church, and some of them who have handled the sacred Word so successfully that they have influenced many in the right way and led them to Christ and His Church, have become inflamed with passion and lust and fallen into the net laid by Satan—undue intimacy with the opposite sex.

We are made to blush with shame as we are compelled to acknowledge the truthfulness of this statement. I must raise my voice against the awful sins and crimes of the past year. The guilty ones as far as are known have been dealt with and put out of the way, but their soul may writhe in hell, and many innocent ones are forced into sadness and distress.

But draw the curtains and hide the scene. It is too unpleasant to keep in the open. Hide it for very shame! I've said enough, you know what I mean. But, beloved, we must take a bolder stand against the evil that forces itself into our very presence.

Listen! Brother, put your hand on that dynamo. Now wait a moment! By means of that dynamo a mysterious power becomes mine—becomes yours. We call it electricity, but no one knows what it is. We only know that if we treat it in the right way, it will enable us to do wonderful things. It will work our mills, and light our houses and our streets and run our cars. It will enable man to do more than any other power that has been discovered. But at the same time, if you treat it in the wrong way, it will strike you dead.

Now, there is another power, very much like it in results. There is a mysterious feeling that men have for women and women have for men. Treat that right and it will bless your life and ennoble it, and make you many times more than you could ever be without it. But treat that feeling wrong, and it will curse you, and blast your life and kill your immortal soul!

Heed the warning and be ennobled by adhering to Paul's instructions to Timothy: Treat the elder women as mothers and the younger as sisters. Be men, be noble men! Have Christian fellowship, but do not become too intimate. And by the grace of God we will rise above the reproach. We will be noble men and women.

The Church shall not suffer defeat and shame on account of the ill conduct of devil-deluded men and women. They must cease their pernicious ways or suffer the consequences. The Church shall not be a cloak to hide such evil practices. If men do not know how to behave themselves and keep in their proper places in their relation to women they are not worthy of membership. If women do not know how to preserve their chastity and honor, and will not do it, they are not worthy of membership. I admit that the woman is the "weaker vessel" and this is all the more reason that the men should exercise enough manhood to both ennoble their own lives and the lives of the women they should protect instead of ruin.

The Church must be a place for protection. The innocent and weaker ones must be protected. We are in the last days, the very time when lust and greed are running rampant, but the Church members shall not be partakers of the nature of the world. They must be pure and holy, and reverence God and love one another with a pure and holy love. There must be a unity of spirit and oneness of purpose, and the shame must be cleared away by a bolder stand for the right. We must be so pure and spotless that one of these days we may hear our Bridegroom say, "Rise up, my love, my fair one, and come away." And by His grace we will!

Division vs Unity

We Should All Speak The Same Thing

GOD HATES THE MAN WHO SOWS DISCORD AMONG THE BRETHREN

Since there is such a determination on the part of the spirit of division to overthrow the spirit of unity, I will write on this important subject. I think of unity as a small force undertaking to come into prominence, and every time it begins to show itself and make its way upward the much more powerful force of division pounces upon it and growls, snaps, tears, pulls and beats the smaller force so terrifically that its life is threatened in a manner that at times it seems there is no chance of recovery.

These are days of division, discord, separation and disagreement. The spirit of discord and divorcement seems to be racing through the world and is getting in its deadly work in every quarter of the globe. It climbs into the legislative halls of all nations, and perches itself on the highest seats of the homes of the people. It prospers in political circles and rides triumphant in broken up homes and divorce courts. And it has the audacity to become prominent in religious circles. It often breaks in where least expected and causes feuds and hellish disturbances. If it were a chemical I would call it some kind of narcotic or nitroglycerine. If it were a place I would name it hell.

This ferocious beast, this deadly poison, this mighty explosive and hell are all united in battle array against unity. And since discord and division exercise such unbounded authority and power the multitudes of mankind fall in with that dominating spirit and fall out among themselves and spend much of their time fighting against one another to their own detriment an deternal loss. Such doings are unwise, to say the least. But that is the way the world is going, and of course we cannot rule the world. The serious thing about division, however, is that it has declared war on unity, and undertakes to exercise such intensive dominating power that unity has but little show, even where it is of the utmost importance for it to reign supreme.

We have pledged ourselves to obey the Bible. The Bible enjoins unity among God's people. The standard for us is unity and we want it. Jesus prayed for it and we want His prayer answered in our behalf. A little further mention of the standard is that we should all speak the same thing, and that there be no division; and that we be perfectly joined together in the same mind and in the same judgment. The Bible is against us having divisions and we must not have them because we took the sacred obligation that we would obey the Bible. And if there are divisions, is not that a sign that somebody is not obeying?

But I think we are getting along nicely now. It would be a serious thing for someone to slip over into the forbidden territory and play the role of our mother Eve when she ate the forbidden fruit. We are told of a certain person that will come around and sow discord. The Bible describes him as "a naughty person, a wicked man." (Prov. 6:12, 14, 16, 19) And it also states that God hates a man that soweth discord among brethren. The Bible also gives special instructions to avoid those who cause division and offences contrary to the doctrine which we have learned. And the doctrine we have learned was given to us by Jesus and His holy apostles. And there is something in our make-up that moves us to continue steadfastly in the apostles' doctrine. It is not our purpose to be moved away from the hope of the gospel which we have heard and received.

Surely we have none in our ranks now that want any more divisions. We feel we have had enough of that kind. O, surely we have none now that would want to sow discord and thus draw the hatred of God upon themselves. I cannot think of anyone now in our ranks that would undertake to cause divisions and by so doing put themselves out to one side to be avoided or shunned by the true followers of Jesus our Lord. I feel that the whispers, backbiters, wire-pullers and political tricksters have all disappeared. We are now in blessed unity. Let us stick together and stick to God and His Bible so closely that the vilest foe will not be able to start the least part of a wedge between us. Paul describes us as being perfectly joined together and compact. Instead of entertaining anything that would have a tendency to separate us in the least degree, let us give attention to that which will draw us closer together.

O, the sweetness of unity! The devil is against it. The spirit of the age is against it. But we are for it. And when I say we are for unity, I mean we are truly for unity as followers of Jesus and Paul. Unity will accomplish something. Unity will produce results. Did you ever read what God said about unity, and the admission He made? Read a few verses and let it have a chance to imbed itself in your minds, and bury itself so deeply in your hearts and lives that it will never disappear, or become extinct.

"And the whole earth was of one language, and of one speech. And it came to pass, as they journeyed from the east, that they found a plain in the land of Shinar; and they dwelt there. And they said one to another, Go to, let us make brick, and burn them throughly. And they had brick for stone, and slime had they for mortar. And the Lord said, Behold, the people is one, and they have all one language; and this they begin to do: and now nothing will be restrained from them, which they have imagined to do." (Gen. 11:1-7)

God plainly states that we can do anything we undertake if we work together in perfect accord and keep out divisions and discord. And since the people were one then as stated in the reading, it is certainly encouraging to believe the Lord's people can be that way again. What has been can be again.

There is a prophecy written directly for the last days that I want to put in here. I think it is worthy of our notice. I think we should give it special attention and keep it as a sacred bit of information in our memory. The devil would try to snatch it away from us. The spirit that is making havoc in the world today would undertake to hide it away until no one would notice it. But the Holy Spirit knew where it was and has uncovered it as He has done many other dark sayings and made it plain to us. God, through the mouth of the prophet said:

"Thy watchmen shall lift up the voice; with the voice together shall they sing: for they shall see eye to eye, when the LORD shall bring again Zion." (Isa. 52:8)

Please notice that the word "shall" occurs in this verse four times. This is the same "shall" that is used by Jesus when He said, "Ask, and ye SHALL receive." "These signs SHALL follow them that believe." And many other places that we dwell upon with such extreme interest and undertake to make so emphatic and forcible.

Considering the last "shall" first we have, viz. "The Lord SHALL bring again Zion." This is an emphatic statement. The word "again" signifies that Zion has existed once before and now the Lord SHALL bring it back again. It is an acknowledged fact that Zion in the Old Testament Scriptures means Church of God in the New. And we all know that the Church of God did exist and was a blessed reality in the days of the Holy Apostles. The prophet plainly states that the Lord SHALL bring it back again to supersede all other churches. And when it is brought back again, "watchmen SHALL lift up the voice," "together SHALL they sing," and "they SHALL see eye to eye."

This is positive proof that the Church of God is to be back in the last days, and its ministers will see alike, speak the same thing, and there will be no divisions among them. The devil says "no," but God's Word says it SHALL be that way. The spirit of the age says "no," but the Bible just keeps on declaring it SHALL. I am going to stick to the Bible no matter how things look. Please notice one more verse of Scripture.

"Brethren, be followers together of me, and mark them which walk so as ye have us for an ensample." (Phil. 3:17)

And I am bold to say that if we follow Paul together, divisions will be a thing of the past among us, and unity will prevail.

Keep in memory that God admits, and states positively, that nothing will be restrained from those who work in unity, or while they are one.

In the face of all this who would dare to step in and undertake to do as has been done in the past and pull off little groups and whisper around in undertones and try to use their influence to create divisions, factions, disturbances, unrest, dissatisfaction, distrust, and prepare for some "filibuster" practices? Such would reap the just retribution of an angry God, just as some have already done, and others who have been caught by the unconquerable avalanche that is slowly carrying them to the same end. I tell you, I would be afraid to do as some have done. I want the favor of God and not the frowns of God. You want His favor and smiles of approval rather than His frowns. I feel an assurance that we have His favor now, then let us keep it by working together in love and unity as we continue the work He has given us to do.

My heart feels melted now with gratitude to God who has chosen us through Jesus Christ to be a peculiar people, zealous of good works. The manifestations of His presence with us, to encourage us on amidst the onslaught of the enemy while the battles have been raging, have been more than wonderful. Kept by His might, power has been realized. His gentle whispers have been an uplift to us more than once when He would say, Be brave, my child, I will never leave thee nor forsake thee.

"Finally, be ye all of one mind, having compassion one of another, love as brethren, be pitiful, be courteous." (1 Peter 3:8)

"Finally, brethren, farewell. Be perfect, be of good comfort, be of one mind, live in peace; and the God of love and peace shall be with you." (2 Corinthians 13:11)

O what a wonderful benediction coming from two wonderful men of God who gave their lives for the very same cause we have espoused!

The World Must Know the Church of Prophecy

God's Name Shall Be Made Glorious In All The Earth

WRONG TEACHING SHALL NOT BE TOLERATED

One reason for our being "churchy" as people often say we are, is because others are not, and the Church of prophecy must be made known. When Jesus built His Church it is reasonable to think He built it to be looked at and talked about. And we surely should not be ashamed of anything He built. It is said also that He built it for an habitation of God through the Spirit, which makes it of vast importance.

The history of its origin and institution has been preserved as if God intended it to be made known. This history was written by the same man that told of the story of the wise men coming from the east in search of the little Baby Jesus, when He was born in Bethlehem of Judea. The record concerning the building of the Church of prophecy out there on the mountain goes everywhere the story of John the Baptist goes. It is carried along with the story of the resurrection. It was written by the same man that gave us the last commission of "Go ye therefore, and teach all nations." It is the only institution that Jesus declared, "the gates of hell shall not prevail against," as told by this same writer, Matthew, one of the Lord's chosen disciples who followed Him until he sealed his testimony with his blood.

It has been said many times that the Church of God of the Bible is God's government for His people on earth. There is much written in that blessed Book to verify that statement. On account of this fact we feel constrained and under strong obligations to talk and teach and instruct about it quite extensively. In fact, I feel strongly impelled to make the Church known in all the world because it is God's government for His people. Because of this, I feel pressed to say the world must know the Church of prophecy. God's people need government just as much as the American people or any other people need government. What would America be without government? What would any people be without government? Without government any people would fall into anarchism and terrorism. Anarchism is absolute individual liberty with no restraint in any way. This is what some religious people call being free. "I am not going to have anybody to rule over me," they say.

Such as this is contrary to the Bible teaching. Thus we say, must know the Church. We could say, must know the government—God's government. God has given a law Book, and in that law Book are laws and rules to govern His people. There are laws given to restrain and there are rules given to encourage and guide the walks and acts of people in a way that will make them a blessing to any community. These instructions tell how to escape hell and how to reach that wonderful heavenly home at the end of this life. But laws and rules are almost, if not wholly, worthless without somebody in authority to see they are obeyed. Thus the Bible makes provision for rulers and governors. These rulers and governors do not necessarily have to govern with an iron hand or cause those under their care or charge to fear in order to hold them in check. But the same Bible that provides for rulers and governors gives instructions to the subjects to be obedient to those who are over them. "Obey them that have the rule over you, and submit yourselves: for they watch for your souls, so they that must give account," says the Book. All of these things are very clear. And this is God's government for His people. This is the Church of God of the Bible.

Israel was Israel in Egypt while they were under the Pharaoh government, but they were not recognized as the Church in the wilderness until God gave them the laws at Sinai to govern them. Church in the wilderness, said the sainted Stephen, the first martyr. (Acts 7:38) It could have been said, God's government in the wilderness. This was theocratic government because God gave the laws and provided rulers with Moses as the chief selected and appointed by God. Our government in the United States of America is a government by the people for the people. But the Church of God is a government by God for His people, and we have God's Word, the Bible, to supply the laws, so this, in fact, is God's government and makes it theocratic.

Yes, ALL MUST KNOW THE CHURCH. And we must teach them until they have learned, and will put everything in operation according to the practices God has been putting His approval on for many years. And since He has put His approval upon it among people of the English language, why may we not expect Him to put His approval upon the same doctrine and practices among people of other languages just the same?

Why the capital of the world for the Church settled at Cleveland, Tennessee, U. S. A.? In the first place, God's providences have placed us here. Why A. J. Tomlinson the General Overseer? This can best be answered by reviewing history. Why the first airplane flown in the extreme northeastern county in North Carolina, U. S. A., and a group of humble followers of Him that spake as never man spake, crawling along on their knees with their Bibles open searching for the Church of prophecy the same year in the extreme southwestern county of the same state and country? Probably we had just as well question about Jesus being born in a stable in Bethlehem. This was according to prophecy, might be said. Yes, but why the prophecy? These things and a thousand more may be without satisfactory explanation, but why raise any question about them? Just as well question about the sun shining by day and the moon by night. It is a continuation of God working everything about the counsel of His own will as Paul has said. Read it:

"Wherein he hath abounded toward us in all wisdom and prudence; Having made known unto us the mystery of his will, according to his good pleasure which he hath purposed in himself: That in the dispensation of the fulness of times he might gather together in one all things in Christ, both which are in heaven, and which are on earth; even in him: In whom also we have obtained an inheritance, being predestinated according to the purpose of him who worketh all things after the counsel of his own will: That we should be to the praise of his glory, who first trusted in Christ." (Eph. 1:8-12)

A mighty fire breaks out in me and that same determination to make God's name glorious in all the world. Yes, people must know the Church, and that it is not like other churches. It must be known everywhere among all nations, peoples, languages and the whole wide world. And Jesus keeps on sounding out the mighty words, EVERY CREATURE. His house must be full! And it is clear that it is going to take more than persuading and letting people do as they please about it. There is the compelling power to be exercised to get those that will not come of their own accord. This way of doing is surely not very far off.

Indeed, God is looking to me for my part in this great drama. He is looking to you—multitudes of men and women —to make this message, this untarnished message—the Scripture rightly divided and kept pure and holy, go into all the world. This is made possible by our watchmen keeping it well guarded and protected. Heresy and unsound teaching SHALL NOT BE TOLERATED. It must be said as much in the last days as in the early days, "And they continued stedfastly in the apostles' doctrine and fellowship, and in breaking of bread, and in prayers." (Acts 2:42)

Wrong teaching and heresy shall not get the pre-eminence over the truth. The watchmen—preachers—must stick to the doctrine that is according to godliness. There must not be a repetition of apostasy as it was in the early Church that caused division and offences contrary to THE DOCTRINE that is held and taught by the Church.

It is not enough to make Christ known in all places of the world, but His Church must be made known also. Not only are the people of every nation, kindred and tongue and peoples, to be saved, sanctified and baptized with the Holy Ghost and fire, but they are to know the Church and be taken into it by covenant, just as you and I came in, where they can be kept also.

Must know the Church! I feel that I should make this as strong and imperative as possible. Compare it with Daniel's stone that is to expand and spread and keep growing and spreading until it fills the whole earth. This is another way of saying that "of the increase of his government and peace there shall be no end." God's Church! God's government! That rock that will break in pieces everything that is mixed with false or rotten doctrine and not sure and steadfast. It will break and tread down everything that is not according to God's plan. This will be done by holding up the true standard rather than by using force in putting down the false. His Church shall be made known in all the earth! Yea, verily, THE WORLD MUST KNOW THE CHURCH OF PROPHECY—THE CHURCH OF GOD!

Responsibility of Pastors

This Is Not The Falling Away Time Described By Paul

WE MUST GET BACK THE LOST MEMBERS AND KEEP THEM

Some one has said that the life of a pastor is filled with sunshine and shadows. That is, he must always appear sunny and pleasant even if he does carry heart-aches and cares. And indeed, he has the care of souls—never dying souls. It is his duty to keep them, feed them, bless them and give account of them.

The Scripture deals quite roughly with unfaithful pastors. God is displeased when pastors become unruly and act and talk or preach contrary to what is best for the flock. A few verses of Scripture may be necessary to show that this statement is true.

"Woe be unto the pastors that destroy and scatter the sheep of my pasture! saith the LORD. Therefore thus saith the LORD God of Israel against the pastors that feed my people; Ye have scattered my flock, and driven them away, and have not visited them: behold, I will visit upon you the evil of your doings, saith the LORD." (Jer. 23:1, 2)

These verses certainly show that the pastors that scatter and drive away, instead of gathering in more, will fall into trouble sooner or later. And this is the time for gathering together instead of a time of falling away. The falling away time that Paul mentions commenced in the year 325 A. D. But now is the time for getting together and pulling together and staying together. The Scriptures are full of teaching to show my statement is true. We must declare war against backsliding and keep the sheep when we get them. The

General Assembly has already instituted the proper plan to keep them and we must do more toward putting it into operation. And the pastors are largely responsible for the functioning of the plan.

A pastor is a shepherd. I have feared sometimes that some pastors are not as careful about taking care of their flocks, who have souls to be saved or eternally lost, as shepherds have been in taking care of their sheep that have no hell to shun or heaven to gain. The eastern custom, as I have been informed through reading and otherwise, is to count the sheep every day so the shepherd may know, without the shadow of a doubt, that all of his sheep are safe. But where are the pastors, even our own beloved and trustworthy pastors, that count their members even once a month and undertake to locate and pray with every one of them? Where is the pastor that checks upon his congregation every Sunday morning to see if they are all present, and if any are missing, goes in search for them on Sunday afternoon or even the next week? (Acts 20:20, 31)

It is my purpose in this message to lay down a line to encourage the pastors, and I want them to know that I feel their duties and work are of the utmost importance for the strengthening and growth of the Church. This is one of my reasons for wanting to encourage and help them if possible to put forth all their strength in taking care of their members. I have been made to feel sick many times when hearing of members being turned out of the Church with scarcely any effort made to reclaim or restore them to favor with God and the other members. I do earnestly hope that kind of business will soon cease, and that the necessary efforts will be made by the pastors in conjunction with the band leaders to save all that go astray, or to prevent their going astray. It is my candid opinion that the greater number of those who went astray and were turned out of the Church could have been kept or won back and saved if the Scriptures were followed and the pastors had done their duty as carefully as shepherds do their duty in counting and taking care of their sheep.

Pastors are given for the perfecting of the saints and not for their destruction. Indeed, there is a grave responsibility upon the shepherds that are recognized as pastors. And God has promised to give the right kind of pastors to help in the great and all-important work of the last days. A few more words from the Bible may be a help right here:

"And I will give you pastors according to mine heart, which shall feed you with knowledge and understanding." (Jer. 3:15)

"And I will set up shepherds over them which shall feed them: and they shall fear no more, nor be dismayed, neither shall they be lacking, saith the LORD." (Jer. 23:4)

These two verses contain much encouragement to our pastors as well as all of us. We have a right to feel that God is giving the right kind of pastors who will not scatter and drive away the sheep or cripple the lambs as has been done by some in the past. And is it not encouraging to our pastors to think of God having given them to be pastors, and that they are God's gift to the Church? If they can only think of it in that way I feel that the position may seem a little more sacred to them. And when the local churches get to feeling that way about it, the members may feel like walking before the Lord and each other with a greater degree of sacredness.

Let me repeat that this is not the falling away time that Paul described. This is not the time for driving away, scattering or losing any of our members. I feel we have been losing too many. We must quit this kind of doing. We must get back all the lost members and keep them. To let them go away now is contrary to God's plan. It is gathering time now. Now is the time to gather in those that have been driven away and turned out. (Ezek. 34:16—first sentence) (2 Thess. 2:1)

I tell you, I am enthused about this. We must fulfil our part of the prophecy and program. And again let me say, and emphasize it strongly, this is the gathering in time—into the Church of God. Now is the time to gather in and then keep them and perfect them—get them ready for the return of our Lord. No more going away after we get them, but hold them fast. There may be some extreme cases that will not fall under this rule, but not many when the doctrine is laid down correctly and all ministers do their full duty and act with wisdom and love. Preaching is not all there is for pastors to do. Their duties and work are of the utmost importance for the growth and strength of the Church. And great care should be taken in the selection of pastors for the incoming year.

I feel that no pastor should be accepted and approved by the State Overseer till he pledges or has already proven his loyalty to the Assembly teachings and rulings. The pastor is to see that all the auxiliaries are organized and kept in fair working order. He should also see that the treasurer makes the monthly reports accurately and promptly. He should also be required to consent to making religious visits to all of his members who live in reasonable distance, and to write letters of encouragement occasionally to those he cannot visit. When these visits are made he should read the Bible and pray with and for them in their homes. And it is also his duty, with the assistance of his band leaders, to hunt up all the strays and keep them when found. He should not limit his visits to the members only, but should also extend his visitations to outsiders for the purpose of getting them interested, saved and in the Church.

When a pastor does his full duty in all these respects there is scarcely any doubt about his being well supported.

Promotion of
Constructive Progress

There is no Alternative But to Win When God And His Bible Are Leading the Way

THE CHURCH IS DESTINED TO MAKE THE GOAL

The superiority of Him who is leading the way makes the landing sure. The inevitable just has to be because there is no way around. When God's Book marks out a line to be traced no oppositions have the power to trip or swerve from the right and proper course. People may falter and turn from the course marked out but God always manages to have enough to carry out His plans and will. This statement is backed up by plainly written words packed in between the lids of the Bible, as well as examples told in story form in the same Book.

I think I never felt quite such a boldness in all my life. I sometimes feel as bold about the work I have been called to do as I imagine Daniel felt when he stepped out before the great king Nebuchadnezzar and declared "the dream is certain, and the interpretation thereof sure." And why not be bold and certain when one knows a thing? What is the excuse for being flimsy and doubtful when there is so much certainty? God has always had His men for the promotion of certain constructive progress. Then why should He deviate from this rule in these last days when the most wonderful piece of constructive work ever attempted is to be promoted?

What was it that emboldened Nehemiah in the promotion of constructive progress in his day? He was in Shushan, many, many miles from Jerusalem when he was told of the walls of that city being broken down and the gates thereof burned with fire. Immediately he was seized with interest and soon on his way to the city to commence the great work that had been laid on his heart. He had only been there three days when he arose at night and went out to make some special investigations. Read a verse of the story given in Nehemiah's own words.

"And I arose in the night, I and some few men with me; neither told I any man what my God had put in my heart to do at Jerusalem." (Neh. 2:12)

There is a secret both of his success and boldness. God was back of him. The work must be done because it was on God's program. Nehemiah was the chosen one for the promotion of constructive progress at that time and there was no alternative but to win when God and His Bible were leading the way. Prophecy had foretold Nehemiah's work and progress and he could be no other way but bold and fearless. Thus his adversaries could not entice him away nor frighten him as they attempted to do. Hear him as he is giving orders to his men when his adversaries sought to hinder the work and prevent it being finished.

"And I looked, and rose up, and said unto the nobles, and to the rulers, and to the rest of the people, Be not ye afraid of them: remember the Lord, which is great and terrible, and fight for your brethren, your sons, and your daughters, your wives, and your houses." (Neh. 4:14)

Please notice how Nehemiah depended upon the Lord. He told of His greatness and magnified Him before the people. His dependence was in Him and not alone in their weapons of war. In another verse he declared that God would fight for them. Yes, Nehemiah knew that he was God's chosen man to master that constructive work and thus he could act bold and defy any thought or action that would have a tendency to engender defeat.

And there is Joshua, another chosen man of God. He could not fail or suffer defeat. But what gave him such boldness about Jericho after he had entered the promised land for which he had journeyed forty years? Read some of the story as it is recorded in our Book of rules. And Joshua was just entering his field for the promotion of constructive progress. He must win. There was no losing in consideration. Nothing but victory could be expected. Thus he could march his great army around the city in full assurance of victory. Only one thing could happen because God had spoken. Read a brief sketch of the story as told by the unerring historian.

"And it came to pass, when Joshua was by Jericho, that he lifted up his eyes and looked, and, behold, there stood a man over against him with his sword drawn in his hand: and Joshua went unto him, and said unto him. Art thou for us, or for our adversaries? And he said, Nay; but as captain of the host of the LORD am I now come. And Joshua fell on his face to the earth, and did worship, and said unto him. What saith my lord unto his servant? And the captain of the LORD'S host said unto Joshua, Loose thy shoe from off thy foot; for the place whereon thou standest is holy. And Joshua did so." (Josh. 4:13-15)

"And the LORD said unto Joshua, See, I have given into thine hand Jericho, and the king thereof, and the mighty men of valour." Josh. 6:2)

Ah, there was the secret of success. There could be no defeat when God said victory. The inevitable must happen because God had told Joshua just what to look for. And it happened just as God had said. Two verses explain the matter—one tells what was to happen, the other tells what did happen. One was spoken before and the other was written after the inevitable had happened. The first was words spoken to Joshua by the Lord and the second was written by the historian. Now read them together:

"And it shall come to pass, that when they make a long blast with the ram's horn, and when ye hear the sound of the trumpet, all the people shall shout with a great shout; and the wall of the city shall fall down flat, and the people shall ascend up every man straight before him." (Josh. 6:5)

"So the people shouted when the priests blew with the

trumpets: and it came to pass, when the people heard the sound of the trumpet, and the people shouted with a great shout, that the wall fell down flat, so that the people went up into the city, every man straight before him, and they took the city." (Josh. 6:20)

"So the LORD was with Joshua; and his fame was noised throughout all the country." (Josh. 6:27)

Of course Joshua could be bold, brave, and certain of victory because he had the assurance that God would be with him. But it was no more the case with Joshua than it was with many others. Moses, his predecessor, had been chosen to lead the children of Israel out of Egypt. This accounts for the untiring efforts and service of that wonderful man of God in going before Pharaoh and pleading with him to let the people go. He knew he was going to be successful before he made his first visit to the king. Thus he continued going time after time, and each time he made some progress and drew nearer to the time of their departure, whether there were any real results seen or not. And thus the statement is always true as given by the apostle Paul who said, "In whom also we have obtained an inheritance, being predestinated according to the purpose of him who worketh all things after the counsel of his own will: That we should be to the praise of his glory, who first trusted in Christ." (Eph. 1:11, 12)

Thus we can say there is no alternative but to win when God and His Bible are leading the way. And there can be no uncertainty about the promotion of constructive progress when the program (God's Bible) shows with certainty what the results shall be. And this is what gives zest and boldness as we pursue the path and program marked out for us. Many have been the movements that have made their appearance in the past thirty years to my own knowledge. I have seen some of them flourish for a while and then disappear until there is now scarcely any trace of their remaining. Others that have started up in more recent years are dwindling. A few that I know of now are at their zenith and if they follow in the wake of others they will soon be out of the way. There is scarcely any hope of people to

thrive in their undertakings unless God is in them and has
marked out the way for their success. Nehemiah knew—
Joshua knew—Moses knew—Gideon knew—and a host of
others knew before they started into their progressive cam-
paigns. Others did not know at the first, but were informed
later on and thus achieved great success.

Insurrection plots have apparently succeeded for a little
while, but ere long their leaders disappear and their cause
lost. Such was true with Absalom when he succeeded in de-
throning his father David. He might have fared much better if he had not undertaken such a wild ungodly scheme.
David was God's man and it was useless and unwise for
anyone, even a son, to undertake to destroy him and usurp
the throne. Absalom perished on short order while David
continued till his work was done. Other insurrectionists
could be named among which was Core who undertook to
undermine Moses while he was engaged in the promotion of
constructive progress. And Core is a constant and solemn
warning to those who undertake to thwart God's purposes
and plans in the last days. To undertake to cause factional
strife, and to build up something that is contrary to God's
eternal program. Jude gives a solemn and powerful warning. Once more I feel like dropping this in for fear some
are still in the land that do not know any better than to
undertake something contrary to God's will as prescribed by
the Bible. This is the class that despises government and
speaks evil of dignities—those God has chosen and anointed
for special work. Read the warning:

"Woe unto them! for they have gone in the way of Cain,
and ran greedily after the error of Balaam for reward, and
perished in the gainsaying of Core. Raging waves of the sea,
foaming out their own shame; wandering stars, to whom is
reserved the blackness of darkness for ever." (Jude 11, 13)

Serious, isn't it, for people to stand out against the right
and become like wandering stars? And when they take things
in their own hands and thus despise government, rule and
authority, they expose themselves to the wrath of God.
They refuse to act according to the advice of those who are
watching for their souls. Some have acted before taking any

time to counsel with those who loved them and were over them in the Lord. Oh, how dreadfully dangerous is such an unwise course! People should hold steadily and be calm and thoughtful at times of extreme temptations and pressure brought upon them by others who are usually arrayed against the very thing that is in harmony with God's will. I tell you, these are indeed perilous times to those who are inclined to be doubtful and unsettled. Such as these should force themselves to stick to those who are established, fixed, settled and certain.

The Church is destined to make the goal. There can be no failure about this. Jesus will present it to Himself a glorious Church, not having spot or wrinkle or any such thing. And who can have the power of authority to prevent it? The Bible plan must be carried out. And this calls for the promotion of constructive progress. Some deep thinking is going on now among the Lord's children. The real sheep that are scattered are becoming more restless all the time. Many of them are still wandering around because they have failed to find what they consider is the true last days Church that is to develop into the one destined to be presented to Jesus. It is my candid opinion that there are many remaining away from us now because they rather hope it will not be us. I believe also that some are almost trembling because they are afraid it is us and that they who, like Paul, have been opposing us and to be right and in that which is destined to make the goal they will yet have to come over and help the very movement they have been opposing. And they will do that rather than fail but they are still standing off rather hoping that it is not us. Such people are to be pitied rather than criticised while they are thus confused. We could help many of them but they will not let us do that yet. But many will come to it later.

While many thousands are confused and in doubt we are still continuing our promotion of constructive progress, all the time knowing that the Church is destined to make the goal, that of being like Jesus. The Scriptures are clear and positive on that point and we are clear and positive that we have found that Church that is destined to make the progress required to reach the state of perfection described in the Bible. I am receiving letters quite often now from honest-hearted and precious people stating that they are fully convinced that we, the Church, is the "it" after all, that will later on measure up to the full standard required and described in the Bible. Of course, we welcome all who come provided they bear the fruits required so we can know them well enough to know they are not deceivers. We always try to watch that point. And our people have been deceived so much they are becoming quite careful about taking in strangers.

I sometimes compare the Church of which we are members with a mighty avalanche slowly sliding down the mountain side. It sweeps everything before it and nothing can impede its progress. With all the oppositions that rise up to hinder or stop the Church and constructive progress, it still moves on as if nothing has ever been in its path to stop it. Our membership is increasing at a fair rate, our ministers are increasing in number almost every day. The interest in all of the helps and auxiliaries is increasing. The W. M. B.'s are doing wonders. The V. L. B.'s are a fiery set almost everywhere you find them. All of these inner forces tell of promotion and constructive progress. Our people have such an amount of holy zeal they cannot be contented without pushing ahead and making progress. This is voiced in every state convention I have attended this year. Everybody wants to help push the work along instead of wanting to be carried along with the tide. Idlers and jokers seem to have disappeared from our ranks. All are in earnest now pressing the work along with thrilling interest. And there are many thrills everywhere I go.

There seems to be an unexplained influence working calmly but surely that will soon bring many more of the sheep this way that have been hindered and kept back by false shepherds. I look for a break to be made soon because the thousands of honest souls cannot be kept back much longer. And God is back of it, for He knows just where the sheep are and He will manage some plan to rescue every one of them. He says in His Bible that He will deliver them from all places where they have been scattered. The mountains, hills and secret places of the stairs will have to give up their prey for God is determined to have every one of them for His Church.

The work is extremely pleasant to us because we know we are destined to win. People may try to make us doubt, but we are too far up the mountain steep now to pay any attention to their stories and influences. We are too busy in the promotion of constructive progress to pay any attention to stories of defeat or discouragement. Yes, we are destined to win. Amen!

In the Preparation Time

The Church of God Doctrine Unchangeable

AGAINST PROGRESSIVE SANCTIFICATION AND "BORN IN THE CHURCH"

Questions and doubts as to the time in God's great drama in which we are living here so completely vanished that we give no place to them. Confidence is strong and powerful. And confidence makes strength. Doubts produce weakness. This is the time to be strong. No time now for weakness in our ranks. Others may be weak but not us. We are to be strong. I repeat it, this is the time to be strong.

We do not boast in ourselves or in our own physical strength, but some kind of a force keeps penetrating our being until we feel compelled to make mention of it and honor our God for supplying it. I believe this strength or force is supplied by His strong and almighty arm. It is pleasing to me to give Him the glory for it all. And by His grace and favor, strength and power we will be all that is required of us in this special dispensational time. My soul floods with joy and a special sense of satisfaction as I make this statement.

God's great drama has been in action constantly for thousands of years. We have read of some of the past, we know some of the present, and we are making special preparations for the future. And a part of the future is so near at hand that we do not have to guess about what it will be. I feel that this is indeed wonderful. And it gives me almost unbounded joy to know, and to some extent at least, realize that we are now in the preparation time; in the time of preparation for the return of our Lord for whom we have been waiting and looking so long.

Confidence, I say, yes indeed, as much, I believe, as David had when he selected the five smooth stones and ran out to meet Goliath. That young stripling of a youth knew the victory was won before he started. He did not consider the size of the opposition forces. He did not regard the boastful words of his foe. On, on, he ran to meet and overcome the big giant. And this he did with perfect ease and confidence because he trusted in his God, the very same God that is now so greatly favoring us—the Church of God. And my heart is exultant with praises to God because He has so wonderfully displayed His power in revealing, guiding, preserving and moving us into this, our part, of His great drama. The most interesting time to live of all ages. And the most wonderful part of the drama to be enacted shortly, and even now we are on for our part in the preparation time.

While we have this pleasure, this confidence, this boldness and strength, others are fulfilling their part in another scene. Jude speaks of them as mockers—imitators. He calls them raging waves of the sea, foaming out their own shame. These are trying to imitate the true and genuine, but they will come to naught. They may fool a few people a little while with their deceivings, but they will not be able to deceive the honest and sincere children of God very long. Imitations or mockings will not be able to stand the acid test.

Jude further describes this class by calling them filthy dreamers who despise dominion or government and speak evil of dignities. He further states that they speak evil of things which they know not. And he goes so far as to designate them as brute beasts, and shows that they corrupt themselves by doing those things. They murmur, they complain, speaking great swelling words apparently trying to bluff somebody with their boastful threats. That is a little on the order of Goliath, but his boastful words and threats had no effect upon David. And people of that type had just as well save their breath because they cannot stop the onward march on God's chosen army. God who worketh all things after the counsel of His own will is caring for His own chosen ones and will see to it that the full preparations are made for the return of our Lord.

The Church of God, the pillar and ground of the truth, has always held to the sacred doctrine of our Lord and Saviour Jesus Christ. In this doctrine is one special point I delight to emphasize because it is ridiculed and spoken against by so many professed followers of the Bible. This point is the one designated as sanctification. I have lived long enough to see many, who once taught this glorious truth, renounce it as a second definite work of grace wrought in the heart, subsequent to regeneration. And this makes me stronger in its favor, because the Scriptures seem to stand out more powerfully than ever. And thus I make the statement that we are as strong for sanctification as ever and no compromise. Many people who claim to believe in sanctification are ready to call it a progressive work to say that they are definitely and wholly sanctified. We are strong advocates of instantaneous sanctification the same as being born again instantaneously and receiving the Holy Ghost instantly and suddenly. (Acts 2:4)

It is to be remembered that letters were written to sanctified people and some of these are on record so we can read them. And if sanctification was an experience to get a little more all the time and never reach the end, then the writers of the letters mentioned above were surely out of place in addressing them to people who were already sanctified. Now read a few verses of this kind.

"Paul, called to be an apostle of Jesus Christ through the will of God, and Sosthenes our brother, Unto the church of God which is at Corinth, to them that are sanctified." (1 Cor. 1:1, 2)

This certainly shows that there were some in the Church of God already sanctified. Of course the true Church of God stands for sanctification, and that sanctification that is already experienced and possessed, and not merely in process of working, that is, progression, or progressive. These people to whom Paul was addressing his letter were already sanctified, the same as the Church of God was already the Church of God. Then it is clear that the Church of God and instantaneous sanctification go hand in hand. In other words, to be the Church of God of the Bible it has to accept the sacred doctrine of sanctification. And with this statement it would not be too much to say that no church, regardless of what name they give it, whether Church of God or any other name, can ever be the real true Bible Church if the members do not accept the doctrine of sanctification that really sanctifies so a letter may be addressed to sanctified people—those who already have the experience. I do not think I make this one bit too strong. And I could not, yea, I would not be, and remain, a member of any church that does not teach sanctification as a second definite work of grace or experience. I would know that such a church could not be the real true Bible Church. And in this same letter Paul states plainly, "but ye are sanctified."

Now we will take a look at another letter that was addressed to sanctified people. I want this to be noted with deep interest. The main reason I want this to be noted so carefully is because so many people are deceived by blinded leaders and all will fall into the ditch together if the innocent ones do not get away from such blind leaders. To me this is serious, and it is my purpose to raise my voice against all sorts of deceptions. And to make it worse, many who claim they are the Church of God reject the doctrine of sanctification as a definite experience subsequent to regeneration. Now read the beginning of the letter to which I refer.

"Jude, the servant of Jesus Christ, and brother of James, to them that are sanctified." (Jude 1)

Now it is clear that this letter was not written to, or addressed to people who were going to be sanctified, or who were progressing on in the direction of being sanctified, but to those who already had the experience. It is the sanctified people that can have peace and love multiplied unto them. It is only to the sanctified people that are preserved in Jesus Christ and called. The people who are always progressing and never reaching the full experience can neither be preserved or called according to this analogy. Neither are they exhorted to earnestly contend for the faith. And this letter is not directed to people who deny sanctification and thus dishonor the blood of Jesus that was shed to sanctify us. Read again:

"Wherefore Jesus also, that he might sanctify the people with his own blood, suffered without the gate." (Heb. 13:12)

Now I wish to call attention to other Scriptures bearing on this subject which show people are already sanctified and not merely progressing toward it as they say. But I wish to show further the close relationship existing between the experience of sanctification and the Church of God. I stated above that people cannot be the true Church of God and disregard sanctification as a definite experience already obtained. Now please notice that the blood of Christ sanctifies, which has already been shown, and the same precious blood has purchased the Church of God. Read:

"Take heed therefore unto yourselves, and to all the flock, over the which the Holy Ghost hath made you overseers, to feed the church of God, which he hath purchased with his own blood." (Acts 20:28)

This is more proof that sanctification obtained because of the shedding of the blood belongs to the Church of God, and that without this glorious doctrine and members in it that are sanctified by the blood, people banded together in some organizations cannot be the true Church of God. And people who do not conform to the glorious doctrine of sanctification, no matter how much they call themselves the Church of God, cannot be **IT**. And I mean sanctification already obtained and not progressing toward it, or in other words, growing into it. No, the Bible sanctification does not come that way. That is too much like the Bible tells of some people "ever learning, and never able to come to the knowledge of the truth"—ever growing up to sanctification and never getting the experience so that a letter can be addressed to people who **ARE** sanctified. If people cannot be sanctified definitely and wholly, as some teach, then Paul and Jude both made a mistake. But we know there was no mistake made by these men of God, and the Church of God doctrine is unchangeable.

Now here are some of the other Scriptures that show with

no uncertain sound that people can be sanctified and do actually have the experience.

"And now, brethren, I commend you to God, and to the word of his grace, which is able to build you up, and to give you an inheritance among all them which ARE sanctified." (Acts 20:32)

"To open their eyes, and to turn them from darkness to light, and from the power of Satan unto God, that they may receive forgiveness of sins, and inheritance among them which ARE sanctified by faith that is in me." (Acts 20:18)

"And such were some of you: but ye are washed, but ye ARE sanctified, but ye are justified in the name of the Lord Jesus, and by the Spirit of our God." (1 Cor. 6:11)

"And the very God of peace sanctify you wholly; and I pray God your whole spirit and soul and body be preserved blameless unto the coming of our Lord Jesus Christ." (1 Thess. 5:23)

"If a man therefore purge himself from these, he shall be a vessel unto honour, sanctified, and meet for the master's use, and prepared unto every good work." (2 Tim. 2:21)

"For both he that sanctifieth and they who ARE sanctified are all of one: for which cause he is not ashamed to call them brethren." (Heb. 2:11)

"For this is the will of God, even your sanctification, that ye should abstain from fornication." (1 Thess. 4:3)

"By the which we ARE sanctified through the offering of the body of Jesus Christ once for all. For by one offering he hath perfected for ever them that ARE sanctified." (Heb. 10:10, 14)

These verses all show very clearly that sanctification is an experience obtained and lived, and not a gradual experience that never ends. We are now sanctified by the blood of Christ. The experience is definite and real, of which the Holy Ghost is a witness. (Heb. 10:15) And this experience must be sought and obtained before the Holy Ghost comes in to dwell. The teaching of the Church of God is simple and clear. And sanctification is not the new birth as some would try to believe and teach. It is not the giving of life but it is rather a death—death to the old man (Rom. 6:6). I want everybody to know that we are as strong for sanctification as ever and no compromise or lowering the standard. The Church of God doctrine is unchanged and unchangeable.

Since we are now in the time of preparation I feel it necessary to keep the doctrine clearly and definitely before the people so none will weaken at the very wrong time. Instead of weakening it is time to become stronger than ever. The compromising or standard lowering spirit is in the world and it is necessary that we meet it with a bold front with no uncertain sound. And that same old poison theory that has been nagging at us for years is still trying to fasten its fangs in some of the weaker ones. I speak now of that deceptive theory that people become members of the Church of God by virtue of their being born again or baptized with the Holy Ghost. Such unscriptural statements must be exposed and met squarely in the face with the Scriptures rightly divided. This is the only safe way. And we must let people know plainly that the Church does not want members that try to bring those spurious theories in with them. We only want those as members that accept the teaching clear and definite in organizing new churches and in taking new members into our ranks. This is very necessary now in this time of preparation, because no lowering of standard will stand the test.

It is clearly stated that the completely ready standard is to be like Jesus. And this standard will never be reached by any manner of retrocession. This standard can only be reached by holding on to the present standard—that is, not lowering it any—and reaching after the next steps that take us a bit higher. This view, or ideal, is upheld by Paul in his wonderful declaration and explanation of standards to which I call special attention here. Read:

"Not as though I had already attained, either were already perfect: but I follow after, if that I may apprehend that for which also I am apprehended of Christ Jesus. Brethren, I count not myself to have apprehended: but this one thing I do, forgetting those things which are behind, and reaching forth unto those things which are before, I press toward the mark for the prize of the high calling of God in Christ Jesus. Let us therefore, as many as be perfect, be thus minded: and if in any thing ye be otherwise minded, God shall reveal even this unto you. Nevertheless, whereto we have already attained, let us walk by the same rule, let us mind the same thing." (Phil. 3:12-16)

This explanation makes it obligatory for us to hold what we have and press on to the higher standards marked out for us when the time is fully come for our Lord to return. We must not drop back, but we may press on to the next higher standards that will be attainable in its dispensational time. And that standard is to be like Jesus. This is voiced by John where he says:

"Beloved, now are we the sons of God, and it doth not yet appear what we shall be: but we know that, when he shall appear, we shall be like him; for we shall see him as he is. And every man that hath this hope in him purifieth himself, even as he is pure." (1 John 3:2, 3)

Peter also contributes more to this same rule when he says:

"Wherefore, beloved, seeing that ye look for such things, be diligent that ye may be found of him in peace, without spot, and blameless." (2 Peter 3:14)

We may be up to the standard marked out for the time of the preparation, but not to the full standard marked out for the time—the exact time of His coming. But we are to walk by the same rule so wonderfully portrayed by Paul. Hence, as stated above, there must be no retrocession, no dropping back to any lower standards that have been passed. We may press on up to the higher but never drop back to any lower. And this is the doctrine and its principles. Then hurrah for the Church of God.

Driving Furiously
Toward the Goal

The Mighty Terrible Company of Two Armies With Banners Will Prevail and Fulfill Prophecy

EASY, RESTFUL PEOPLE TO TURN FRANTIC WITH INTEREST

I declare to you that that "I can't sit down" spirit has got such a hold on me that I can't sit down or let anybody else sit down with any satisfaction. How can I rest easy when certain work is to be done to fulfill prophecy that is now almost within our grasp? Who that has caught the vision can drive leisurely along when it is going to take furious driving to run in on schedule time? I tell you, I'm afraid and really scared as I think of the multitudes yet unawakened. We surely must be the army the Bible tells about that is to make its appearance in the latter days to arouse and awaken the multitudes who are unawakened.

But we ourselves will have to be fully awakened before we can awaken others. I feel right now that I would like to have a man with a fife and two big boys with drums. Be like the drummer boy that was asked to beat a retreat. He said he could not beat a retreat. He said he could not beat a retreat but insisted that he could beat a charge that would cause the dead to fall in line. That is what I want with a fife and the two drums. There must be some plan invented to awaken many of our own people. They must every one be lined up in battle array. The uncomely members must be dressed up in a way to make them comely. The feeble and weak members must be made strong and powerful. Every member must become a worker.

"Nay, much more those members of the body, which seem to be more feeble, are necessary: And those members of the body, which we think to be less honourable, upon these we bestow more abundant honour; and our uncomely parts have more abundant comeliness. For our comely parts have no need: but God hath tempered the body together, having given more abundant honour to that part which lacked: That there should be no schism (division) in the body; but that the members should have the same care one for another." (1 Cor. 12:22-25)

This is getting every member harnessed up and pulling his part of the load. This is getting every member to be a worker. This is one aim we have while we are driving furiously toward the goal which we are bound by prophecy to make on schedule time. Get it! O, beloved, get it! Get the vision! Get the full import of these words and what is meant by the furious driving to make the goal on schedule time. And indeed it will take furious driving to run in on time. And to stir our people to do their best is my reason for wanting the fife and drums. Joel tells us to blow the trumpet, and I want that, too. Anything it takes to awaken our people so we can drive furiously through the land to awaken others. And we must have every member a worker in order to make the most successful drive.

Surely I must have caught the last days spirit and I want everyone to catch it. Surely I must have heard some of the Lord's counsel. I am into it with all my heart. Others are into it also. We have surely heard the voice of the great head of the Church. He must be directing the movements. We recognize Him as our Chief Shepherd. I feel almost furious now as this message goes forth. Why shouldn't I when such values are at stake, and the goal has to be reached on time? Let Jeremiah help me a little right here. Read:

"For who hath stood in the counsel of the LORD, and hath perceived and heard his word? who hath marked his word, and heard it? Behold, a whirlwind of the LORD is gone forth in fury, even a grievous whirlwind: it shall fall grievously upon the head of the wicked. The anger of the LORD shall not return, until he have executed, and till he have performed the thoughts of his heart: in the latter days ye shall consider it perfectly." (Jer. 23:18-20)

I am considering this thing, and I see that we must become affected with the same kind of furiousness that Jeremiah tells about. This is not a mad, mean furiousness, but that kind that makes us want to drive our work furiously to make the goal on time. And I declare we will have to do this or fail, and by the grace of God we will not fail. We must, we must, we will, we will make the goal on time. The mighty terrible company of two armies with banners will prevail and fulfill prophecy. We have to take this gospel of the kingdom to every creature. It is shown that we have to go into the houses, on the houses, in the holes of the rocks and every place where they may be in hiding—but we have to find them.

I started to go into a house one day, and as I was about to enter the front door the family ran out at the back door. I did not run after them, but I deliberately took possession, sat down and waited till they all returned, then I gave them the message with love and tears. God was with us, and gave the victory. The terror that struck the family as I entered was turned to rejoicing. We may frighten people as we drive furiously through the land, but often people need to be frightened before they will listen to God's messengers. The last days are here and we are considering the whole thing just as marked out by Jeremiah. We must keep our furious driving until easy, restful people will turn frantic with interest. This is no time to let people rest easy. There is too much to do and too few to do it. We can't spare any to let them lie around idle.

I used to sit and talk with people about this thing in order to show them courtesy. But it makes me feel miserable to do that now. I feel like time is too precious to spend it that way. Everything must be business now—business for God and to keep up the furious driving for souls. I feel that I must keep racing back and forth before the army after a similar manner practiced by General Grant in the Civil War to instruct, encourage, keep the drums beating and the trumpets blowing. This is for the purpose of getting every member lined up as a worker and puller.

I have had a vision before me for years about lining up our people in a drive in Tennessee from east to west which would result in covering the entire state and putting the message in every home. This is not practicable yet, but I don't think it will be long until we can single out a county and make a thorough canvass of a state by counties. We will have to get into this kind of work soonor or later and I wonder how far in the future until this kind of organized work will start.

I once heard of an eighty-five mile stretch of road being graded in a day. This was done by gathering in the people on either side of the line on a certain day. Every man had a tool to work with and every man did his part of the work. By this hearty co-operation and every man a worker the work was done. This is the way we can get our work done, but it is going to take some furious driving because the time is so short and the work is so great.

The word terrible—why is it used? The Bible uses it in connection with the armies with banners. The word is also used in describing the works of the Lord as well as Himself. A few verses will explain, read them and see.

"O clap your hands, all ye people; shout unto God with the voice of triumph."

And this helps to explain why we are so bold and certain about our work and what we will do. And we both clap our hands and shout like we have the victory and have triumphed already. Well, we can do this because the prophecies are sure—we must make the final dash that will put us to the goal on schedule time. Now read more of this Psalm.

"For the LORD most high is terrible; he is a great King over all the earth. He shall subdue the people under us, and the nations under our feet." (Psa. 47:1-3)

"And said, I beseech thee, O LORD God of heaven, the great and terrible God, that keepeth covenant and mercy

for them that love him and observe his commandments."
(Neh. 1:6)

"O God, thou art terrible out of thy holy places: the God
of Israel is he that giveth strength and power unto his people. Blessed be God." (Psa. 68:35)

"And in thy majesty ride prosperously because of truth
and meekness and righteousness; and thy right hand shall
teach thee terrible things." (Psa. 45:4)

"But the LORD is with me as a mighty terrible one: therefore my persecutors shall stumble, and they shall not prevail: they shall be greatly ashamed; for they shall not
prosper: their everlasting confusion shall never be forgotten."
(Jer. 20:11)

Why shouldn't I use the word terrible when God Himself is with me as a mighty terrible One as well as He was
with Jeremiah? Why shouldn't I be bold and certain when
I am sure the Scriptural prophecies will be fulfilled and
that we are in His eternal program? But let us have more
Scripture references to assist in explaining our reason for
the statement—the mighty terrible company of two armies
with banners will prevail and fulfill prophecy. This was
used in prophecy to describe the early Church when the
question was asked thus:

"Who is he that looketh forth as the morning, fair as the
moon, clear as the sun, and terrible as an army with banners?" (Cant. 6:10)

And the early Church was both mighty and terrible.
When they had been forbidden to preach any more it was
acknowledged by the very men that had forbidden them
that they had filled Jerusalem with their doctrine. And after
they got away from the court they continued their work
both in the temple publicly, and in every house personally.
They preached the very name from the use of which they
had been enjoined. They were terrible as an army with banners. At Thessalonica the people had a fear of the terrible
army when it arrived in their city. Those who were so
frightened began to call for help against the invasion of their
city and cried out against them by saying:

"These that have turned the world upside down are come hither also." (Acts 17:6)

Some arrests were made, but still that early Church army marched on and on preaching the very name they had been enjoined from using. They just could not keep from it. Indeed the early Church was the terrible army with banners of which it had been prophesied about seven hundred years before. Fear and dread of it filled the country until it was accused of turning the world upside down. That was the early Church, but what about the latter Church that is on hand now? Of the last days Church it is said, "As it were the company of two armies." The early Church was terrible as an army with banners, and the latter Church is to soon become terrible as a company of two armies—God's host.

In the light of all of these Scriptures, and the analogy given, I am not exaggerating or using deceit when I say, the mighty terrible company of two armies will prevail and fulfill prophecy. And indeed we are driving furiously toward the goal with a full determination to reach it on schedule time. We know we will have to hurry and this accounts for the high speed at which we are running.

"Mighty terrible." What words! What an expression! What do the words mean, and what does the expression mean when the two words are put together? "Mighty terrible." How odd this sounds! "Turn the world upside down" sounds odd, too. "The company of two armies" also sounds odd. So we will admit that the early and latter Church is an odd set. Odd means singular, singular means peculiar, and peculiar applies to we who are so zealous for the cause we have espoused.

"Looking for that blessed hope, and the glorious appearing of the great God and our Saviour Jesus Christ; Who gave himself for us, that he might redeem us from all iniquity, and purify unto himself a peculiar people, zealous of good works." (Titus 2:13, 14)

For our assistance in gaining knowledge and understanding of these words which combine to create an odd expression let us proceed to define the words. Mighty means—powerful; strong; influential; momentous; wonderful; huge; having might of force; courageous; vast; violent; tempestuous; excellent; high.

Terrible means—dreadful; formidable; exciting; dread, fearful; powerful; frightful; exciting or causing fear or awe; reverence; a sense of profound admiration and respect.

All of these definitions combined make a structure that can scarcely be overthrown and which I consider impregnable—that is, not to be captured, not be overcome. And this agrees with Jesus who said that "the gates of hell shall not prevail against it"—His Church. That is, this mighty terrible company of two armies with banners shall not be dedefeated, but will continue driving furiously to make the goal against all the odds; against all the oppositions and hindrances that may be thrown across their path to stop their forward march. Hallelujah! Now if I had the fife and drums, and the trumpet to sound, I would surely put them to use as we march on to final triumph, and certain victory.

And the goal—this has been expressed, but a rehearsal will serve to make it stronger.

"This gospel of the kingdom shall be preached in all the world for a witness unto all nations." (Matt. 24:14)

"Teach all nations, baptizing them in the name of the Father, and of the Son, and of the Holy Ghost: (We will have to baptize all of them that have been baptized in Jesus' name only, and a lot of others, too). Teaching them to observe ALL THINGS whatsoever I have commanded you." (Matt. 28:19, 20)

"The perfecting of the saints . . . and of the knowledge of the Son of God, unto a perfect man, unto the measure of the stature of the fulness of Christ." (Eph. 4:12, 13)

"Warning every man, and teaching every man in all wisdom; that we may present every man perfect in Christ Jesus." (Col. 1:28)

"Preach the gospel to every creature." (Mark 16:15)

"And to make all men see." (Eph. 3:9)

"Let us be glad and rejoice, and give honour to him: for the marriage of the Lamb is come, and his wife hath made herself ready." (Rev. 19:7)

"We know that, when he shall appear, we shall be like him." (1 John 3:2)

"When Christ, who is our life, shall appear, then shall ye also appear with him in glory." (Col. 3:4)

"And when the chief Shepherd shall appear, ye shall receive a crown of glory that fadeth not away." (1 Peter 5:4)

"That he might present it to himself a glorious church, not having spot, or wrinkle, or any such thing; but that it should be holy and without blemish." (Eph. 5:27)

"For the Lord himself shall descend from heaven with a shout, with the voice of the archangel, and with the trump of God: and the dead in Christ shall rise first: Then we which are alive and remain shall be caught up together with them in the coluds, to meet the Lord in the air: and so shall we ever be with the Lord." (1 Thess. 4:16, 17)

O, what a goal! Who would not think it is worth striving for? Who would not think it worth driving furiously to obtain? Who would want to work for this goal and be so slow at it that they would not get in on schedule time? I think to be a few minutes behind would be a catastrophe, a calamity, a disaster. I can't think of such a thing, therefore, I am driving furiously for the goal, and I mean to keep up the fife blowing and drums beating and trumpet sounding to awaken the people everywhere. And I mean to awake them, too. I do not expect to let them rest and lazy along as they draw out—"D-o-n'-t b-e i-n s-u-c-h a h-u-r-r-y, t-h-e-r-e i-s p-l-e-n-t-y o-f t-i-m-e y-e-t." I feel like doing like the angels did to Lot and his wife and two daughters to get them out of Sodom.

"And when the morning arose, then the angels hastened Lot, saying, Arise, take thy wife, and thy two daughters, which are here; lest thou be consumed in the iniquity of the city. And while he lingered, the men laid hold upon his hand, and upon the hand of his wife, and upon the hand of his two daughters; the LORD being merciful unto him: and they brought him forth, and set him without the city. And it came to pass, when they had brought them forth abroad, that he said, Escape for thy life; look not behind thee, neither stay thou in all the plain; escape to the mountain, lest thou be consumed." (Gen. 19:15-17)

O that this message and the power of the Holy Ghost may cause easy, restful people to turn frantic with interest and climb into the swiftest chariot and join me in driving furiously toward the goal. I feel I must get our people so aroused that every member will be a worker, tithe payer and giver. O God, put this message home! Amen!

Build the Church—
Every Member Saved

Calling All Workers To Promote This Great Campaign

HELPING THE LORD FIND HIS SHEEP

People are sometimes compared to sheep in the Bible. Jesus frequently calls His people sheep. He speaks of Himself as the Shepherd of the sheep. He tells of a man having a hundred sheep and when he learned that one was lost he left the ninety-nine and went in search of the one that was lost, and never stopped till he had found it. The one he went in search of was a sheep, but it had gotten separated from the balance and was lost. The owner would not try to be satisfied with having the ninety-nine close around him and probably all in good condition. No, he could not rest until he had found the other one and brought it home with the others. He must have his full hundred.

Peter tells of some people who were as sheep going astray. These were left with no shepherd to guide them and keep them together, or prevent their going into places of danger, and wandering so far away that they could not get back. I see them going now with their heads down, nibbling the grass as they go, unsuspecting of any danger. There they go from one little green spot to another. Perhaps the grass is not as good and sweet and juicy as that where they had been accustomed to feeding, but it is grass anyway, and perhaps the next place will be better. So on they go, making their rounds from one place to another until they get so weak that they scarcely have strength and courage enough to attempt to go back home, even if they know the way. Thus, instead of attempting the long journey they try to content themselves where they are, lose their good spiritual experience and finally join one of the popular churches and try to subsist on wire grass the balance of their days.

The first time these "going astray" people stepped aside and went over to that other place they had no intention of going again or of going to any other place later, but when they got there the people gave them such a hearty welcome and took so much pains to show them kindness and when the meeting closed the minister and others gathered around them and talked so pleasantly and urged them to "be sure and come back," they decided to go again. And sometimes when they do come back home they tell how nice they were treated at the other place and how the people over there seem to love them better than their own folks at home. But that is a start in going astray. And people who are isolated and away from home are often caught in that kind of snare. And even sometimes when people have all the opportunities of good wholesome spiritual food among the right kind of people they slip off to other places of meeting because they say they want a little change and in doing this they often inhale enough poison to sap the spiritual life out of them and soon fall away and die spiritually. A sheep already back in some of the wire grass fields that has never known any better pasture may be able to subsist a good while, but a sheep that has had the very best kind of picking from infancy will soon starve to death in the wire grass fields.

It is Ezekiel that tells about the Lord searching for His sheep and bringing them out from the people. He tells how they have been scattered among the different societies or organizations but the Lord is going to get them out of such places and put them in His Church, where they rightly belong. The prophet tells of the wanderings of the sheep, or rather states that they have wandered through all the institutions and governments, and Jeremiah states that they have gone from mountain to hill—from the big institutions to the smaller ones and that they have even forgotten their resting place. (Jer. 50:6) They don't know the Church of God is the place for their rest. This prophet calls them lost sheep and yet they are the Lord's people. And it is happiness to know they are to be brought back from all the places where they have been scattered into their own resting place. This is voiced by many Scriptures and the sheep had just as well get ready for the journey. When the Lord undertakes to do a thing He is sure to accomplish it, and the prophecies cannot fail. Yes, the Lord is finding His sheep. Many are scattered about over the mountains starving for spiritual food and they must be found, brought and fed among the many who are already enjoying their resting place.

Ezekiel's expression, "I will bring them out from the people," shows very clearly that not all the people are sheep. And it is the sheep only that the Lord is going to bring. It is clear, then, that the sheep will hear the voice of the Shepherd, but the people will not. To the people Jesus says, "Ye believe not, because ye are not of my sheep." Then He distinctly states, "My sheep hear my voice, and I know them, and they follow me." Now there is the difference. His sheep hear His voice and follow Him and the people who refuse to follow Him are not worthy of being designated as sheep. Very few of the people who are in the popular churches know anything of repentance and being born again any more and therefore they do not hear His voice as He calls out repentance. They don't hear His voice about sanctification. They don't hear His voice about the baptism of the Holy Ghost with the other tongues as the evidence. They don't hear His voice about His church with the apostles' doctrine and fellowship. Ask them about many of these points of teaching and they answer that they do not believe in them. What is the reason they don't believe in these points of teaching when they all came from the sacred lips of Jesus? Let Jesus answer: "Ye believe not, because ye are not of my sheep." (John 10:26) Then follows His statement which I give again, "My sheep hear my voice, and I know them, and they follow me." (John 10:27)

Taking this view of it then, it does not seem so difficult for the Lord to find His sheep. Those who follow Him are His sheep and those who are not will not follow. They will not even hear His voice as He calls. Thus the sheep will be brought out from among the people and into their resting place. They hear His voice as He calls by the Bible and by the Holy Ghost and they follow Him.

But what about some who appear to follow well for a while and finally draw back, disappear and are gone? John explains this far better than I can when he answers, "They went out from us, but they were not of us; for if they had been of us, they would no doubt have continued with us: but they went out, that they might be made manifest that they were not all of us." (1 John 2:19) They look like sheep, they talk like sheep, they act like sheep and they think they are sheep, but by their going away shows they are not sheep. Such things as this are hard to understand, but I do not worry over them like I used to. If they are sheep they will continue with us, or if they wander off a while they will come back, and if they are not sheep it is good that they go.

Several years ago a certain gentleman came into the Church of God because he was "so delighted to find a people who accepted the whole Bible rightly divided." He worked along with our people, but quite often I would hear of some friction and conflict. This kept going on and we bore with him until the break came in 1923. Conditions were such that his membership fell on the "other side." He became dissatisfied and requested that his membership cease entirely. And still he could not be satisfied. He put in his application for membership with us. I was rather favorable to receiving him, but knowing of past frictions I was rather slow. Time passed on and still he was not in, yet he still kept pressing his application. At last I asked him his reason for being so anxious to join when we seemed to disregard his request so much. He replied that he liked the Church of God because it stood for the whole Bible rightly divided. And further on in the conversation he stated that he saw our imperfections and he wanted in to help us on toward perfection. That was all very well, but then I began to draw on him for a further explanation and what he wanted to add or subtract from our practices. It did not take long for me to learn from him a lot of things that he wanted to introduce and force into practice that were contrary to the apostles' doctrine. I finally told him that if that was his idea he need not expect us to receive him.

But he kept right on begging, but I still said no, and finally told him that as long as he held to the views he had expressed it was useless for him to say anything more about it. I say, let such people go off and start something of their own if they want to and not be trying to interfere with the work God is calling us to do—follow Jesus as a sheep and hear His voice in whatever He says unto us. (Acts 3:22) We have not crawled along on our knees and searched the Scriptures together for these many years for nothing. Some wild graftings have been injected a few times which have caused us much trouble and we do not want any more. We want the plain Word of God and to follow the Voice of Jesus as He calls, and nothing else will satisfy. I feel like walking carefully and softly before God and making every step solid and sure. I want to be such a close follower of Paul in his teaching and practice that I may be worthy of the mark of good stewardship.

I feel there is much need of extreme carefulness in these days. Every kind of a fad and wind of doctrine is being presented to lure the Lord's people away from the path marked out by Jesus and His holy apostles, but the words of Jesus still remain true, "My sheep hear my voice, and I know them, and they follow me." If His sheep are going to hear His voice and follow Him why do we need to be so concerned and worried when some people take the opposite direction and constantly ignore His tender voice and pleadings? True, if they are sheep we want them with us, but if not, then we had better let them go their way, for if they remain they will give trouble sooner or later. Sheep get along together very well, but wolves in sheep's clothing will sow discord and pave the way for dissension and trouble even if they do not directly cause it themselves. Jesus gives a solemn warning concerning this class when He says, "Beware of false prophets, which come to you in sheep's clothing, but inwardly they are ravening wolves." (Matt. 7:15) But on the other hand, we do not want to get so fearful over reports of wolves in sheep's clothing that we will reject the sheep when they come. Jesus says that we can know them by their fruits.

Call attention to Peter's statement about some who were
as sheep going astray. Peter's epistle is represented as being general in its application. With this in view it might
not be wrong for the most of us to acknowledge our part
of Isaiah's statement where he says, "All we like sheep have
gone astray; we have turned every one to his own way,"
and then add the last part of Peter's verse and apply that
to us also. Read, "but are now returned unto the Shepherd
and Bishop of (our) souls." And if this is a prophecy of
happenings of the last days, which is very probable, it shows
a time when the sheep will have returned. And this view
is agreeable to Jesus' statement where He says, "Other sheep
I have, which are not of this fold: them also I must bring . . .
and there shall be one fold, and one shepherd." (John 10:16)
Agreeable to this also is another one of Peter's statements,
where he repeats from Moses saying, "For Moses truly said
unto the fathers, A prophet shall the Lord your God raise
up unto you of your brethren, like unto me; him shall ye
hear in all things whatsoever he shalt say unto you." (Acts
3:22) This prophet referred to is Jesus. His sheep will
hear His voice and they will follow Him. And Peter, in his
statement, gets clear over on the other side and declares
that though they had been as sheep going astray they have
now returned. He sees them already returned. Ezekiel says
the Lord will search them out from all places where they
have been scattered and bring them out from the people into
the place where they belong; Jesus says He MUST bring
them so that there will be one fold and one shepherd; He
also says His sheep will hear His voice and follow Him, and
Peter leaps away over and sees them after the search has
been made, the sheep found and returned.

To me it is quite encouraging to know Peter got a vision
of the work ended and the sheep returned. This is like
Peter's statement about healing through Jesus. Isaiah saw
into the future and stated that Jesus would heal the people,
or how healing should be accomplished through Him and
said, "And with his stripes we are healed." (Isa. 53:5) But
Peter climbed away over on the other side and said, "By
whose stripes ye were healed." (1 Peter 2:24) Now since
we can be healed by the power of Christ and we gain courage,

faith and strength for healing because Peter said, "By whose stripes ye were healed," increases my courage, faith and strength in regard to the Lord finding His sheep and getting them into His fold because Peter says, "For ye were as sheep going astray; but are now returned unto the Shepherd and Bishop of your souls." (1 Peter 2:25) Now since Peter saw the thing already accomplished I have a right to see it the same way. And with all the divisions and oppositions that make such a thing appear impossible I can go through them all with courage and boldness, declaring that the inevitable will come, for prophecy must be fulfilled.

I have been settled on this subject for years, but this discovery adds more proof. And when I have full proof back of me I can "laugh at impossibilities and cry, It shall be done," just as our forefathers have done. The statement is true. I am delighted with it and thus once more repeat it with increased confidence and certainty. "The Lord finding His sheep. Many are scattered about over the mountains starving for spiritual food, and they must be found, brought and fed." People who oppose this truth are only wasting their breath and strength. Peter leaps over all the isms, divisions, perils, false brethren, heretics, truce breakers and traitors, with all the winds of doctrine that increase to hurricane, tornado and cyclonic proportions, takes his stand upon the everlasting Word of God and while standing there openly and boldly declares that the sheep have followed their Shepherd and returned. My faith in this is so strong— that God's sheep from every place where they have been scattered will be brought to the Church of God—that I can say, like was said of the faith of Abraham concerning his son, Isaac, when he was about to slay him at the command of God, "Accounting that God was able to raise him up, even from the dead; from whence also he received him in a figure." (Heb. 11:19)

The Last Days
Church of God

I wish to call attention first to the goal as shown by the apostle Paul in his letter to the Church at Ephesus. The text I shall start with reads, "This is a great mystery: but I speak concerning Christ and the church." (Eph. 5:32)

The goal for which we are striving and which must be reached, is stated in verse twenty-seven, but in order to make it clear I wish to read a few verses preceding as an approach to the goal referred to. In explaining this subject the apostle uses the husband and wife and their relation to each other. And bear in mind that he is not trying to give instructions to the husband and wife, but states clearly that he is referring to Christ and the Church. Now read the verses.

"Wives, submit yourselves unto your own husbands, as unto the Lord. For the husband is the head of the wife, even as Christ is the head of the church: and he is the saviour of the body. Therefore as the church is subject unto Christ, so let the wives be to their own husbands in every thing." (Eph. 5:22-24)

With no further explanation or reading it would appear that Paul is here giving information concerning the husband and wife and their relation to each other exclusively and using Christ and the Church to illustrate. But it is right the reverse. And verse thirty-two corroborates my statement. In this chapter Paul is explaining what it takes to make the Bible Church. It is obedience to Christ in everything. And any body of people who does not conform to the doctrine of Christ and obey Him in every thing cannot be the Bible Church. Even if they call themselves by the name, Church of God, they are not the Bible Church unless they obey Him in everything.

These verses then could read, submit yourselves unto Christ, because He is the head of the Church and the Saviour of the body, therefore the Church is subject unto Christ in every thing.

This rendering does no violence to Paul's teaching because he clearly states that he is speaking about Christ and the Church and not so much the husband and wife. However, in using the husband and wife to illustrate the relation of of Christ and the Church, Paul does give some good instructions to husbands and wives and their relation to each other.

It is clearly stated that the Church of God is subject to Christ, its head, in everything. He is the giver of the laws or commands that govern the members of the Church. And with these commands or laws there are rules to show how to deal with the unruly and disobedient. Just because one member disobeys or refuses to comply with the rules does not destroy the fact that it is the Church of God that stands for obedience to Christ in every thing, any more than if a citizen of the United States, becoming disobedient to the laws of the land, destroys the government of the United States.

Now we want to consider the next three verses. Read:

"Husbands, love your wives, even as Christ also loved the church and gave himself for it; That he might sanctify and cleanse it with the washing of water by the word, That he might present it to himself a glorious church, not having spot, or wrinkle, or any such thing; but that it should be holy and without blemish." (Eph. 5:25-27)

Another verse follows that adds weight to the statement here that Christ gave Himself for the Church. Read:

"Take heed therefore unto yourselves, and to all the flock, over the which the Holy Ghost hath made you overseers, to feed the church of God, which he hath purchased with his own blood." (Acts 20:28)

Jesus having purchased the Church of God, as Paul explains in both verses, He further reserves the right to cleanse it. This shows that it is the Church of God before it is clean and spotless. It also shows that some of the members may not even be holy, and may have some blemishes. And this gives rise to our practice of taking people into the Church as members who are only converted. The Word is to be used by the ministers to regulate the lives of the members and lead those who are not holy into holiness. The apostle mentions this process as a washing of water. Water is used to wash dirt off of floors, streets, your hands and everything. So the Word of God is used to clean up the lives of the members who are not yet clean and pure. Agreeable to this explanation are other verses which you may now read.

"And he gave some, apostles; and some, prophets; and some, evangelists; and some, pastors and teachers; For the perfecting of the saints, for the work of the ministry, for the edifying of the body of Christ: Till we all come in the unity of the faith, and of the knowledge of the Son of God, unto a perfect man, unto the measure of the stature of the fulness of Christ: That we henceforth be no more children (to get in the dirt,) tossed to and fro, and carried about with every wind of doctrine, by the sleight of men, and cunning craftiness (I learned long ago to stay away from places where I was liable to hear false teaching,) whereby they lie in wait to deceive; But speaking the truth in love, may grow up into him in all things, which is the head, even Christ: From whom the whole body fitly joined together and compacted by that which every joint supplieth, according to the effectual working in the measure of every part, maketh increase of the body unto the edifying of itself in love." (Eph. 4:11-16)

All of these verses show that there may be members in the Church of God that have defects from which they may be delivered through the faithfulness of the ministers and the power of God. And all the time these defects are there the organization is still the Church of God. But at the same time the Church of God stands for the whole Bible rightly divided, and the New Testament as its only rule of faith and practice. That is, it is subject to Christ in everything without any reservations. All of these operations are to take place, and keep on working until the high state of perfection is reached as described in the following verse which agrees to the one already mentioned and will be repeated below.

"Let us be glad and rejoice, and give honour to him: for the marriage of the Lamb is come, and his wife hath made herself ready." (Rev. 19:7)

All of these processes of cleansing and washing and removing defects by the Church itself (she makes herself ready), until the time Jesus comes for it.

"That he might present it to himself a glorious church, not having spot, or wrinkle, or any such thing; but that it should be holy and without blemish." (Eph. 5:27)

THIS IS THE GOAL toward which we are moving. It is false and wrong for any one to say he belongs to the glorious church not having spot or wrinkle. There is no such a thing, and will not be, until "His wife hath made herself ready" by the processes described. And when she is ready—fully ready—He will come for her and take her to Himself as already stated.

But a question was raised about a spiritual church composed of all saved people. My answer was, There is no such teaching in the Scripture. The Church of God is just as real as the government of the United States. Its laws are on the statute books, they can be obeyed or violated. Its members are to have a spiritual experience, and the more spiritual the better, but the members themselves that obey or violate the laws and rules are more than a spirit.

The bosh or fallacy of a spiritual church composed of all saved people in all churches of our day, or out of any church, is shown by the following words of Jesus. Read:

"Moreover if thy brother shall trespass against thee, go and tell him his fault between thee and him alone: if he shall hear thee, thou hast gained thy brother. But if he will not hear thee, then take with thee one or two more, that in the mouth of two or three witnesses every word may be established. And if he shall neglect to hear them, tell it unto the church: but if he neglect to hear the church, let him be unto thee as an heathen man and a publican." (Matt. 18:15-17)

There is scarcely any need for comment on this Scripture because anyone can see that telling it to that so-called spiritual church with no definite membership is an absurdity. And the Bible recognizes no such a nonentity as being the Church of God.

Another question was raised as to who would be in the rapture as the Church of God, which is destined to be presented to Christ by Himself when He comes for His bride. Many believe He will get some here and some there from all the different churches and independent "saints." But their opinions do not change the Word of God. It still remains that He will present the Church to Himself, and does not say the good people of every church or no church. The fact is, such people are looking at present conditions under present systems, and not at conditions as they will exist when His wife (not wives) hath made herself ready, and the Scriptures already referred to fulfilled. Those Scriptures tell how the people are to be brought together into "one body, with one Lord, one faith, one baptism." (Eph. 4:5, 6) The work is to be carried on by the Holy Spirit and ministers "till we all come in the unity of the faith, and of the knowledge of the Son of God, unto a perfect man (not men), unto the measure of the stature of the fulness of Christ." (Eph. 4:13) All of this finished, and just one Church, under one government, and all subject to Christ in everything, which it takes to make the Church of God. I aver that this will be the condition when the Church of God is raptured away by our Lord. You cannot even imagine that the Lord will rapture away people who will not obey Him when He requires that the Church be subject to Him in everything as it approaches the time for presentation. And that time is now. That is, we are rapidly approaching the time for presentation.

After we have been marking out the goal for which we are striving, we will now turn back to prophecy which points out the establishing of the Church, its establishment, some of its work, name, and give further proof of what it takes to be the Church of God, by referring to words spoken by Jesus Himself in reference to the subject. We will take up prophecy first. Prophecies and their fulfillment are interwoven with other material and subjects so that the natural man may not be able to pick them out and put them together correctly. The Holy Spirit reserves the right to give the interpretation of the Scriptures. This is evidenced by Paul and Jesus. Let them speak.

"But the natural man receiveth not the things of the Spirit of God: for they are foolishness unto him: neither can he know them, because they are spiritually discerned." (1 Cor. 2:14)

"At that time Jesus answered and said, I thank thee, O Father, Lord of heaven and earth, because thou hast hid these things from the wise and prudent, and hast revealed them unto babes." (Matt. 11:25)

An example as proof is given in the prophecy which tells where Jesus was to be born. (Micah 5:2) The statement is also verified by the meager prophecies concerning Judas who betrayed Christ. (Reference to this is given at Acts 1:16-18; Psa. 69:25; Psa. 109:8) Others could also be given. And some of the Scriptures are mixed up by placing last verses first and first verses last as well as clauses and sentences in one verse. And I might add that chapters are often put in out of the regular order. But the Holy Ghost had charge of the whole, while the different writers told just what the Holy Spirit directed. And it takes the whole to make the chain complete.

Now let us turn to some prophecies which tell of the founding of the Church. Then we will call attention to their fulfillment. First, the prophecy. Read:

"And it shall come to pass in the last days, that the mountain of the LORD'S house shall be established in the top of the mountains, and shall be exalted above the hills; and all nations shall flow unto it. And many people shall go and say, Come ye, and let us go up to the mountain of the LORD, to the house of the God of Jacob; and he will teach us of his ways, and we will walk in his paths: for out of Zion shall go forth the law, and the word of the LORD from Jerusalem." (Isa. 2:2, 3)

Another prophecy by Micah reads almost the same, except some of the sentences are transposed, and a few words changed. But it is evident that the two prophets are telling beforehand of the same thing—the founding of the Church. Read Micah 4:1, 2, with Isaiah 2:2, 3.

Now look for the fulfillment in the New Testament Scriptures. There are portions of three chapters that might be considered. But these are also interwoven with other information so they are liable to leave the reader mystified if he is not guided by the Holy Spirit. Bear in mind that this is still a "mystery which hath been hid from ages and from generations, but now is made manifest to his saints." (Col. 1:26) And the Lord has ordained that men are to see what is the fellowship of the mystery that has been hid so long, and that the Church may know the manifold wisdom of God. (Eph. 3:9, 10)

After saying this much about the mixtures of Scriptures to be unraveled and made plain by the Holy Spirit, and of the mysteries that are to be known by the Church of God, and probably hidden from others, we call attention to the founding of the Church by Jesus Himself subsequent to the statement that He would build His Church. Now read:

"And he goeth up into a mountain, and calleth unto him whom he would: and they came unto him. And he ordained twelve, that they should be with him, and that he might send them forth to preach, And to have power to heal sicknesses, and to cast out devils." (Mark 3:13-15)

The four verses following give the names of the first members. This record shows that the names of the first members were recorded. Then it is definitely known that Judas Iscariot was made treasurer because it is plainly stated that Judas carried the bag. Read John 12:6 and 13:29. It would appear here by the reading that the first thing in order was the ordination service. But there is the same mystery again. Jesus had already told them that He was going to build His Church. He had shown them the difference between building on creeds and something positive, made so by revelation and two positive statements. (Matt. 16:13-18)

To assist in building up this part of the structure, and as further proof that the twelve names were the first members, please notice that when the disciples had repaired to the upper room to await the downpouring of the Holy Ghost, it is said that 'the number of names together were about an hundred and twenty." (Acts 1:15) Here is evidence of an increase of membership. This time women are mentioned as members. And special mention is made of Mary the mother of Jesus. (Acts 1:14) And after the Holy Ghost had been given and three thousand people saved, and doubtless sanctified and filled with the Holy Ghost, it is said that still more members were added to the Church. (Acts 2:47)

It is untrue that the "Church was started at Pentecost," as some try to teach. It had to be started at some previous time for others to be added as they were. If there had been no Church then these would have been added to nothing. But the Church was founded by the Lord out upon the mountains as stated above, which is agreeable to the prophecies given. The prophets did not say that the house of the Lord would be established in the upper room, but instead they said "that the mountain (government) of the Lord's house (Isa. 2:2) shall be established in the top of the mountains." So it is clear that Jesus started the Church while He was still with His disciples, had their names registered as members, appointed or selected a treasurer, ordained twelve, and set them to work. I might add here that it is evident that the prophecies of Isaiah and Micah referred to have a two-fold meaning and I have only referred to one. This statement is verified by Peter who says that "no prophecy of the scripture is of any private interpretation." (2 Peter 1:20)

To further verify some of the statements made and give additional information concerning this great institution and its early existence, go with me to that wonderful prayer of our Lord as recorded in the seventeenth chapter of John's gospel. Please remember that Jesus said He would build His Church. Now in this prayer He says among other things:

"I have manifested thy name unto the men which thou gavest me out of the world: thine they were, and thou gavest them me; and they have kept thy word." (John 17:6)

Here is a positive and direct statement that they had been true to their covenant made when they were set together in the Church. They had kept His word. And this agrees with the statement above that the Church of God is subject to Christ in everything. He says these men, the very start of nucleus of the Church, had faithfully kept His word or been subject to Him in everything. Then He has manifested His Father's name unto them, that is, Church of God. He had called it His Church but He named it after His Father instead of Himself. And He being the founder had a perfect right to give it a name. And this is agreeable to prophecy again which reads:

"Thou (Zion) shalt be called by a new name, which the mouth of the Lord shall name." (Isa. 62:2) And He named it Church of God and then prayed thus, "Holy Father, keep through thine own name those whom thou hast given me . . . While I was with them in the world, I kept them in thy name . . . And I have declared unto them thy name, and will declare it." (John 17:11, 12, 26) Here then is the Church of God, the name of which Paul takes up in his writings and refers to so frequently. The Church of God at Corinth, feed the Church of God, and other similar references. And Jesus kept them in that name till He finished His work.

We have considered the goal for which we are striving and which will be reached in due time. We have also considered the origin or founding of the Church of God. We show that in the ending the Church is subject to Christ in everything to be the Bible Church. We also show that this was the standard at the beginning. We have not dealt with the middle ages, but one verse of Scripture is in order here. Read Rev. 1:8.

Here is an acknowledgment that Jesus was obeyed, and His words were faithfully kept at the beginning of the Church and will be kept at the ending. But we know by history that He was ignored in between. And this view is clearly taught by the prophets which show that the Church will arise out of the debris and slime of the "dark ages," creeds and unbelief and shine forth brilliantly in the last days until it is suddenly glorified—transformed into the glorious Church and Jesus presents it to Himself.

It is a precious theme to me. My soul is now on the wing as I look forward to the rapid approach to the goal—A GLORIOUS CHURCH, NOT HAVING SPOT, OR WRINKLE, OR ANY SUCH THING.

The Love That
Loves and Wins

There Is A Depth Of Experience Yet To Be Attained That Will Be Effective Always

DIG DEEPER AND CLIMB HIGHER

I have just been poring over some problems that must be mastered. I am reminded of the way I used to pore over my lessons in my school days. Those problems in mathematics had to be mastered and I could not think of giving them up and saying to the teacher next day, I can't. I felt that I must win and I did. Some of them were tremenduously hard for my immature mind to master, but there were only two things for me to do; back down and be put to shame before my classmates and teacher, or dig into it and get the correct answers. Well, without discussing that subject further I chose the latter even if it was hard.

I still have many problems before me, and they must every one be mastered. I refuse to be mastered by anything that I should master. I may not win in a day, or perhaps not in a week or months, but I am not to allow myself to give up. It has taken years to master some problems that look easy now, and one wonders why it could not have been done at the first without so much effort. But that is not always the way the hardest problems are mastered.

One of the special problems that is up for solution is the one that deals with the question of keeping souls after they have been won for Christ and become members of the Church. Almost constantly members are becoming neglectful, disobedient, and sometimes rebellious. They seem to lose sight of the acute vision they had of themselves and the importance of salvation. They seem to forget the danger of being lost as they realized it when they first gave their hearts to God. Outside influences seem to cause some of them to cool off and lose the fervency of spirit that they once enjoyed. I think it is a serious thing for people to look back after they have started in the right way. To keep all the members in constant service for the Master so they will not become dull and disinterested is one of the problems that must be mastered.

There is a depth of love into which everyone should be plunged that will furnish such attractions, power and interest until they will be so shielded from outside influences that they will not be affected thereby. Love is a keeping power. Love is a preserving element. Love for God and love for souls will succeed in the Christian race when everything else fails. And there should be no failure in living the life for God after once escaping from the entanglements of sin and getting a touch of the divine hand of God. The wise man exalts the value of righteousness and the power of love when he says, "The mouth of a righteous man is a well of life: but violence covered the mouth of the wicked. Hatred stirreth up strifes: but love covereth all sins." (Prov. 10:11, 12)

The apostle Paul in his love chapter verifies my statement when he shows what love will and will not do. And he carries Solomon's statement farther on when he gives the following account of love:

"Charity (love) suffereth long, and is kind; charity (love) envieth not; charity (love) vaunteth not itself, is not puffed up. Doth not behave itself unseemly, seeketh not her own, is not easily provoked, thinketh no evil; Rejoiceth not in iniquity, but rejoiceth in the truth; Beareth all things, believeth all things, hopeth all things, endureth all things. Charity (love) never faileth." (1 Cor. 13:4-8)

This is truly the love that loves and wins. It can be clearly seen by Paul's statement and explanation that there is a depth of love into which everyone should plunge that would give him a victorious and progressive life as a Christian. Solomon says that love covereth all sins. Then by plunging into that fountain of love no sins can be seen because they are covered. And it was the love sacrifice of Jesus that opened that fountain into which everyone may plunge so his sins may be covered by the precious, cleansing blood of the Lamb. Then when one is hidden in this fountain of love he will suffer a long time and still be kind. He will never misbehave and act or talk contrary to what a Christian should. He will neither be selfish or selfwilled. This means he will take the advice of those who are over him in the Lord and watching for his soul. He will take no pleasure in iniquity, but will rejoice in the truth. And Paul concludes by declaring that love will never fail. This goes to show that he that is constantly bathing in that fountain of love will never fail either in living the right kind of a life or rendering successful service to the Master.

In this love message, I am referring to the love that really and truly loves and wins. The apostle Paul indicates that there is a kind of "make believe" love that is nothing but deceitfulness and hypocrisy. Of this he says, "Let love be without dissimulation"—hypocrisy. (Rom. 12:9) But this does not prove that there is not a true and genuine love in which one may live. It was the true love that Jonathan and David had for each other. It is the true and genuine love that is going to love and win. It is the real, the true, the genuine that cannot fail. O God, give us this love that will win in the Christian race and pull others out of sin and put them on their feet for God. Of Israel, God said, "I drew them with cords of a man, with bands of love: and I was to them as they that take off the yoke on their jaws, and I laid meat unto them." (Hosea 11:4)

Israel was often rebellious, and sacrificed to Balaam, and burned incense to graven images, and still God would manage some plan to get them back. History shows this was repeated many times over, but the love of God was longsuffering and kind and took them back when they repented. He "drew them with bands of love." And although Israel often forgot God, yet He was still after them to do them good. What wonderful words of love are these spoken to those who had wandered away from God, and ceased to serve Him as they should.

"The LORD hath appeared of old unto me, saying, Yea, I have loved thee with an everlasting love: therefore with lovingkindness have I drawn thee. Again I will build thee, and thou shalt be built, O virgin of Israel: thou shalt again be adorned with thy tabrets, and shalt go forth in the dances of them that make merry. Therefore they shall come and sing in the height of Zion, and shall flow together to the goodness of the LORD, for wheat, and for wine, and for oil, and for the young of the flock and of the herd: and their soul shall be as a watered garden; and they shall not sorrow any more at all. Then shall the virgin rejoice in the dance, both young men and old together: for I will turn their mourning into joy, and will comfort them, and make them rejoice from their sorrow. And I will satiate (satisfy fully) the soul of the priests with fatness, and my people shall be satisfied with my goodness, saith the LORD." (Jer. 31:3, 4, 12-14)

And this is God's dealings with Israel and is prophetical or illustrative of what He is going to do for His people and the Church in the last days. God loved with an everlasting love. He is still the same today. Then those who have the love that loves and wins will surely have this everlasting love. As more proof on this subject read, "Beloved, if God so loved us, we ought also to love one another. No man hath seen God at any time. If we love one another, God dwelleth in us, and his love is perfected in us. And we have known and believed the love that God hath to us. God is love; and he that dwelleth in love dwelleth in God, and God in him. Herein is our love made perfect, that we may have boldness in the day of judgment: because as he is, so are we in this world." (1 John 4:11, 12, 16, 17)

It is not strange then about the power of love. It is not strange about the love that wins. God is love, and the love that wins is God. God would not rest satisfied while Israel was backslidden and doing contrary to His orders. When we have this love that wins, God dwelleth in us and we cannot be contented to let our brethren—our members—go astray without going after them and bringing them back.

David, the shepherd boy, keeping the sheep for his father

saw a lion rush into the flocks one day and snatch a sheep and run away with it. David would not rest—could not rest with one sheep being carried away in the jaws of a lion. Quicker than thought David made a dash for the lion. He did not hesitate long enough to even think of his own life being in danger. No, he must have the sheep, and no time to stop and reason, because the lion was running away with the sheep. David ran after him with a determination to have his sheep. When he came up with him he lost no time in the rescue. He smote the big old shaggy lion and then David had a fight on hands. But David "caught him by the beard, and smote him, and slew him." He did the same for the bear. He rescued both of the sheep or lambs.

While the lions and bears are running off with our sheep—the members—are we just going to go on with our songs and rejoicing without making any effort to rescue some that are torn and mangled by the devil and his agents? No! A thousand times, no! The love that loves and wins will not let us rest until the wandering ones are brought back and safely cared for in the fold. The love that loves which dwelleth in us will not let us rest until the lambs are delivered from the clutches of Satan and brought back and put in the Sunday School class, in the prayer meeting, in the V. L. B., or W. M. B. We must have every member. We may be accused of being beside ourselves on account of the interest we show in rescuing the strays, but that makes us that much like Paul who said, "For whether we be beside ourselves, it is to God: or whether we be sober, it is for your cause. For the love of Christ (love that loves and wins) constraineth us." (2 Cor. 4:13, 14)

Then the apostle Paul continues by showing whom we are and what we should and must do.

"Now then we are ambassadors for Christ, as though God did beseech you by us: we pray you in Christ's stead, be ye reconciled to God." (2 Cor. 4:20)

As long as they are members they are ours, and we must feel responsible for them. When the lions and bears undertake to carry them off we must run after them and never stop till we get them and bring them back. This statement is illustrated by the story given by Jesus of the hundred sheep. And in that story the shepherd never stopped till he had found the sheep that was lost. And please also notice that it was not enough to simply find the lost sheep, but he took it back home with him and had a jubilee time of rejoicing when he got there. He raised the neighbors and had them to help him rejoice. If a sheep that has no soul is worth so much, how much more is a lost man or woman worth that has a soul?

I tell you kindly, beloved, I am afraid we are taking things too easy in this respect. I am afraid we are not fully awake yet to our responsibility as shepherds and sheep tenders. I am afraid we have not become so interested in the souls of some who have gone astray as to be accused of being beside ourselves while we are searching for them. I fully believe there is a depth of experience yet to be attained that will be effective always. And we will find them all and bring them back to the Christ that gave His life for them. Listen to John as he tells the good news.

"My little children, these things write I unto you, that ye sin not. And if any man sin, we have an advocate with the Father, Jesus Christ the righteous: And he is the propitiation for our sins: and not for ours only, but also for the sins of the whole world." (1 John 2:1, 2)

Now since we are ambassadors, personal representatives of Christ, our duty is surely very clear. Go after them and take up Paul's plan if they have gone so far away as to require it. Paul was after his people who were "fallen from grace." (Gal. 5:4) He meant to get them back and here is what he said:

"My little children, of whom I travail in birth again until Christ be formed in you." (Gal. 4:19)

This reads like he meant to have them back, and that he did not mean to stop till they were born again and Christ formed in their lives the second time. There is persistence for you. There is determination. I must grapple with the lion and the bear and wrench my sheep from their mouths. These had been saved, but they had fallen from grace. They must come back again through the new birth, and Paul infers here that he had no other alternative but to bring them back. I tell you, beloved, it is surely time for some of us to dig deeper and climb higher when the tremendous responsibilities of lost souls, whether sinners or backsliders, are resting so heavily upon us. We will surely need the very highest grade of experience marked out by the Bible for service in these last days.

I do not know just how you are feeling about the matter, but I feel that we cannot afford to stop short of being in full possession of that love that sure enough loves and wins. And John tells it about like Paul, if I can read the Scriptures right. Paul said his Church of God members had fallen from grace—probably not every one—but a number of them. Then he indicated in his letter that he was not going to exclude them, but he was going to hold on to God in prayer and soul travail till they were saved over again. Now hear what John says about saving or reclaiming backsliders. "If any man see his brother sin a sin which is not unto death, he shall ask, and he shall give him life for them that sin not unto death." (1 John 5:16)

This was what Paul meant, and John means to pray and travail until Christ is formed in them. These are real examples. Don't exclude such as these, but pray, work, persuade, weep in soul travail, until their hearts will be broken and repentance is made and salvation takes possession. This is some of the effect of the love that loves and wins. This may call for digging deeper and climbing higher in experience, but surely, beloved, no time should be lost and no strength spared to save a soul from hell.

And this is one of the problems that I feel must be mastered—getting our ministers and other workers so interested in the backsliders that they will go after them and never stop till they are brought back unless they have sinned the sin unto death spoken of by John in his verse already referred to.

I believe with all my heart that there is a love that really and truly loves and that love will win. I also believe there is a depth of experience yet to be attained for our last days work that will always be effective. Let us dig into it. Let us climb up to it. Let us be sure that we attain to the very experience marked out by the Bible for us at this special time. I feel that we must make advancements in consecrations in order that these deeper experiences may be reached.

All the disciples were baptized with the Holy Ghost on the day of Pentecost. But later on they got together and held another prayer meeting and prayed till the "place was shaken where they were assembled together; and they were all filled with the Holy Ghost, and they spake the word of God with boldness." (Acts 4:31)

This was digging deeper and climbing higher, was it not? Suppose we undertake something on this order to increase our boldness in giving out the Word both publicly and from house to house.

"And with great power gave the apostles witness of the resurrection of the Lord Jesus: and great grace was upon them all." (Acts 4:33)

And this is the love that loves and wins. Amen!

Christian Heroes Are Needed

We Must Win In This Great Struggle For The Right

TO BE WEAK NOW MEANS TO BE LED ASTRAY BY EVIL FORCES

"O, Lord God Almighty, the Father of thy beloved and blessed Son Jesus Christ, by whom we have received the knowledge of Thee, the God of angels and powers, and of every creature, and of the whole race of righteous who live before Thee, I give Thee thanks that Thou hast counted me worthy of this day and this hour, that I should have a part in the number of Thy martyrs, in the cup of thy Christ, to the resurrection of eternal life, both of soul and body, through the incorruption imparted by the Holy Ghost. Among whom may I be accepted this day before Thee as a fat and acceptable sacrifice, according as Thou, the ever-truthful God, hast foreordained, hast revealed beforehand to me, and now has fulfilled. Wherefore also I praise Thee for all things, I bless thee, I glorify Thee, along with the everlasting and heavenly Jesus Christ, Thy beloved Son, with whom, to Thee, and the Holy Ghost, be glory both now and to all coming ages. Amen."

This was the prayer of our beloved and sainted father, Polycarp, after he was bound to the stake, surrounded by wood and fagots, just before the funeral pile was set on fire which was to burn him in martyrdom for his invincible faith and truth in Jesus Christ. He had been faithful in life, now he wanted to be faithful unto death. Others had been martyred in Smyrna and now he was the twelfth. He had been a hero in life and now he is to be a hero in death. He had boldly declared himself a Christian in the face of threats of punishment. When the proconsul threatened him with wild beasts to devour him if he did not repent he urged him to "call them then, for we are not accustomed to repent of what is good in order to adopt that which is evil; and it is well for me to be changed from what is evil to what is righteous." But again the proconsul said to him, "I will cause thee to be consumed by fire, seeing thou despiseth the wild beasts, if thou will not repent." But Polycarp said, "Thou threatenest me with fire which burneth for an hour, and after a little is extinguished, but are ignorant of the fire of the coming judgment and of eternal punishment, reserved for the ungodly. But why tarriest thou? Bring forth what thou wilt."

While he spoke these and many other like things, he was filled with confidence and joy, and his countenance was full of grace, so that not merely did it not fall as if troubled by the things said to him, but, on the contrary, the proconsul was astonished, and sent his herald to proclaim in the midst of the people, "Polycarp has confessed that he is a Christian." This proclamation having been made by the herald, the whole multitude both of the heathen and Jews, who dwelt in Smyrna, cried out with uncontrollable fury, and in a loud voice, "This is the teacher of Asia, the father of the Christians, and the overthrower of our gods, he who has been teaching many not to sacrifice or to worship the gods." When the multitude could not get the wild beasts turned upon him then they cried out with one consent, that Polycarp should be burnt alive.

When all was ready and Polycarp had pronounced his amen after his prayer, those who were appointed for the purpose kindled the fire. And as the flame blazed forth with great fury, those to whom it was given to witness it, beheld a great miracle, and were preserved that they might report to others what then took place. This is so wonderful that I give the description in the language of the historian.

"For the fire, shaping itself into the form of an arch, like the sail of a ship when filled with wind, encompassed as by a circle the body of the martyr. And he appeared within not like flesh which is burnt, but as bread that is baked, or as gold and silver glowing in a furnace. Moreover, we perceived such a sweet odour coming from the pile, as if frankincense or some such precious spices had been smoking there. At length, when those wicked men perceived that his body could not be consumed by the fire, they commanded an executioner to go near and pierce him through with a dagger. And on doing this, there came forth a dove, and a great quantity of blood, so that the fire was extinguished; and all the people wondered that there should be such a difference between the unbelievers and the elect, of whom this most noble Polycarp was one."

God is the same God that He was in the days of the early Church when Polycarp was bishop of Smyrna. Christian heroes are as necessary now as then. They were beginning to build upon the foundation of the apostles and prophets, we are to continue the work and finish it up ready for presentation to Jesus Christ when He comes for the Church without spot or wrinkle. The question arises, Will we be as faithful as the early fathers? Will we be as loyal and heroic when the difficulties arise and the persecutions come thicker and harder? But there should be no question for we must! Somebody will, even if we should weaken, but by the grace of God we will not weaken, we will endure the suffering, glory in the cross, scale the heights of heroism, withstand the violence of the fiery spirit that is set to seduce God's children and lead them astray and deceive them until they will be ruined forever. Some may be caught now. The web may be woven around them, and the deadening chloroform of deception may have already gotten in its work, but those who are yet free should lift up their heads, throw up breastworks of protection, and rise above every artifice of the devil by declaring wholly and unflinchingly for truth, righteousness, and freedom, as boldly and bravely as did our forefather Polycarp.

We are now in the last days that are to try the metal in every man to prove what sort it is. If a man can be seduced at all he will be seduced now. Jude's certain men are getting in their deadly work in all the world. False Christs and false prophets are now on their job just like Jesus said they would come. Many are showing signs and wonders and speaking great swelling words to seduce all who are not so fixed and settled that they can bear the name of the elect. All but the elect will be seduced and driven into strong delusion and such a halter placed upon them that they will never get loose any more. Evil men and seducers are now waxing worse and worse, deceiving and being deceived, just like Paul prophesied. Many of those who have been our own people are now in the gall of bitterness because they were not able to stand out against seducing spirits. But all who have been able to stem the tide and ride the waves of doubts and fears are higher in spirituality and fuller of God-given courage and boldness than ever before.

Who would not want to be a hero now? Who would not want to heed the clarion call by the great Apostle Paul when he said, "Watch ye, stand fast in the faith, quit you like men, be strong"? (1 Cor. 16:13) To be a weakling now means to be seduced and led astray. To be discouraged now means to give up the very job that God called you into years ago. To fall behind the main ranks now is to be captured by the advance guards of the enemy that are always picking up stragglers. I prophesy that some who have been good men will soon die and their bodies will be laid in the cold, cold grave, all because they have become confused and have not been able to bravely breast the storm of battle arrayed against them.

It has been said that the best way to withstand the enemy in a defensive battle is to wage a strong offensive battle. Just merely to try to live is to join the ranks of those who are strong and bold in their declamation of truth and right. You must really quit yourselves like men and be strong or be swallowed up by that spirit that is ready to overwhelm and devour every weakling.

Paul commands to withdraw from proud people who will not consent to wholesome words and to the doctrine which is according to godliness. Such people are dangerous because they are possessed by a spirit of strife, envy, railings, evil surmisings and suppose that gain is godliness. To withdraw from such people as a means of protection to keep from falling into the same snare. Paul also insists that the saints of God should turn away from people who are covetous, boastful, trucebreakers, false accusers, traitors, heady, and highminded, although they may have a form of godliness.

Indeed these are perilous times when men are going to be caught in the coils of deception and so strangled by the powers of flattery and otherwise that they will never escape. If I should fail in everything else I do not want to fail to inspire courage and bravery in the soldiers now on the great battlefield against sin and deception. Have courage, my brothers, my sisters, we must win today in this great struggle for the right.

A story is told of one of the generals during the revolutionary war which is very impressive. The odds were against the American forces and the time drew on for another battle. This general addressed his men early in the morning and said, "Boys, we must win today or Mollie Stark is a widow." His gallantry and bravery in the battle caused his men to put forth all their strength. They ran into the fight with undaunted courage and the foe was vanquished and the brave general was not even wounded in battle, and his wife was not left a widow. Surely we can have the same kind of courage in this revolution which is of such vast importance just now.

One Heart and One Soul

Perfectly Joined Together In The Same Mind And In The Same Judgment

JESUS PRAYED THAT ALL MAY BE ONE

It is believed that the deep spirituality that was experienced by the early disciples was the cause of their being so closely united that it could be written of them by the historian that they were all of one heart and one soul. This statement shows they were in close relation with one another in our way of understanding the expression. And Dr. Luke, the writer of this bit of history, states that there was a multitude of them. There were one hundred and twenty, three thousand, and the five thousand. This makes a total of eight thousand, one hundred and twenty definitely named. There might have been more. Probably most of this number had never seen each other before. Entire strangers, but something had happened that caused Luke to write that they were of one heart and one soul.

With such a mass of people it is hardly thinkable that they could have formed a personal acquaintance with each other. But the power and grace of God had so welded them together until "one heart and one soul" described the condition of that vast multitude. This means there was not a word of discord. I think they must have measured up to Paul's requirement when he wrote to the Corinthian Church and beseeched them to be perfectly joined together in the same mind and in the same judgment. This condition can only exist when they are dominated and governed by the same spirit. And this must be the same Holy Ghost of the Bible.

As I dwell upon this part of the subject I feel that I want to nestle close to the same Holy Ghost that came upon the twelfth day of January, 1908. He was real to me then and He is still real. Why shouldn't He be when He took possession of my vocal organs and sang, and talked with them according to His will. I could only listen. I felt the movements and heard the voice and He talked in this way with no effort on my part. This same Spirit that enveloped and took charge of me has the power to operate others also. This Spirit having the power over that vast number, they could be nothing else but of one heart and one soul. This was wonderful. One heart and one soul. Since it was true then it can just as well be true now.

I have long ago decided to be in perfect accord with Job when he cried out exultantly, that he knew God could do everything. Oh how well I know that God has not lost His hold on this world. Like He said to the ocean waves, thus far and no farther, He can say to all men and they have to stop or bend and take a different course. But it is the people of God that are to become one heart and one soul. I have seen this condition verified in many instances on a comparatively small scale. But is it not a fact that such a condition shall exist on a large scale in due time to fulfill the Scripture prophecies? This is what I am looking forward to, and to this end I am working.

Paul undertakes to tell us that this unity shall be brought by the ministers as they teach and instruct. I would not cross Paul for anything. He says the evangelists and pastors and teachers are for the perfecting of the saints and for the building up of the body of Christ. And they are to continue their work till we all come in the unity of the faith and of the knowledge of the Son of God, unto a perfect man, unto the measure of the stature of the fulness of Christ. What wonderful experience! And Paul declares that the ministers shall continue till this state of the perfection is reached. This statement by Paul is enough to make one feel like running through a troop and leaping over a wall. Paul, do you know what you are talking about? Yes, you do. And your word shall not fall to the ground. It must come to pass. You have some close followers who are performing exploits and pushing along at a rapid rate of speed toward the goal.

Paul says to keep on teaching and instructing till we all come to the unity of the faith. Paul, I want to obey your instructions with my part of it. I know I am not supposed to do all of it myself, but what a vast multitude is working with me. Many are men wondered at. Many wonderful women are just as zealous and determined as the men. We cannot think of anything else but working mightily to carry on the work that Paul laid out for us to do. I feel the Samson strength rise up in me. The Book says of Samson and the Spirit of the Lord began to move him at times. That is the way I am moved mightily at times, but never quit even when I do not feel so much of the moving of the Spirit. Obey the Word sometimes whether I feel so much or not. But when the Spirit anoints in perfect harmony with the Word, it is wonderful and all activities are delightful.

One who was riding in an airplane told me a few days ago that the trip was made with the wind and thus the time was shortened. Our moving with the prophecies is like the plane sailing with the wind. Thus the work will move along so that we are sure to reach the goal in due time. And to show that this condition spoken of by Paul is to be reached while there is corruptness we only have to read the next verse which tells of winds of doctrine, cunning craftiness and deceivers still in the world. Read the verse: "That we henceforth be no more children, tossed to and fro, and carried about with every wind of doctrine, by the sleight of men, and cunning craftiness, whereby they lie in wait to deceive." (Eph. 4:14)

How marvelous this is: The Church taught and edified till we all reach that state of perfection that will take us out of the child state, so no one will be tossed about but all will be steadfast and unmoveable. The high state of perfection is also shown by Paul's "unto the measure of the stature of the fulness of Christ." I can scarcely comprehend, or even imagine, millions of those who compose the Church of God having such whiteheated love that there will never be a cross in our teaching. And the millions will be scattered over the world carrying this one heart and one soul experience. The Spirit will surely handle the situation as

perfectly as God controls the inhabitants of heaven. I seem
to feel that atmosphere of love that will dominate everybody in the Church at that time. Paul describes it further
when he says, "But speaking the truth in love, may grow
up into him in all things, which is the head, even Christ:
From whom the whole body fitly joined together and compacted by that which every joint supplieth, according to
the effectual working in the measure of every part, maketh
increase of the body unto the edifying of itself in love."
(Eph. 4:14, 16)

Now notice a little of what Paul says here in these verses.
There is a getting together until the multitudes speak the
same thing and have the same judgment. There is just one
Church at this time. All under one government—the Bible
government. The teachers teaching or speaking the truth in
love and growing with as much reality as the corn grows in
the spring and summer. Then Paul declares it is the whole body
that is growing. Not a member is to be sickly or raise any
disturbance. Nobody can raise any disturbance. It is the
growing time that Paul is talking about. We have not reached
the fullness of the growing time yet.

However, every Christian that is healthy in a spiritual
sense will grow. But Paul here is referring to the time when
the whole body is fitly joined together with every member
operating in his place. Paul speaks of the members as being joints. "By that which every joint supplieth," he says.
And that he means every member is verified by another
verse, thusly: "Nay, much more those members of the body,
which seem to be more feeble are necessary." (1 Cor. 12:22)
The feeble or weak ones are to be taught and trained along
with the stronger ones until all become strong together.

Please notice Paul says "the whole body," not any part
left out. Not a member lost. Everyone in his proper place.
No jealousy existing, but the whole machine running in perfect order to increase and build up itself in love. This surely
means to get more members and put them in training to
make them just like the others. What else could it mean?
Get more members until the house is full. Get all and teach
and train all, till we all come in the unity of the faith.

This means perfect agreement, which is like we say the Church stands for—the whole Bible rightly divided. No divisions in doctrine or anything else. In fact, the multitudes will be of one heart and one soul. No matter where they are in the world they will be alike, they can't help it, they have to come to oneness. The teachers that teach in love will make them come to it.

Our schools in the land teach the same thing until we can hold an intelligent conversation with people we never saw. The work of going into all the world and teaching is imperative. We have to do it. Jesus commissioned the eleven disciples, and they carried the message to others, and on and on for centuries until now it has come to us. Oh, what are we in, since Jesus has spoken with no uncertain sound to us when He said, "Go ye therefore, and teach all nations, baptizing them in the name of the Father, and of the Son, and of the Holy Ghost: Teaching them to observe all things whatsoever I have commanded you." (Matt. 28:19, 20)

This teaching and the teaching of Ephesians must be the same. And this teaching is to continue and be the kind that will bring the multitudes to the unity of the faith, and to the measure of the stature of the fulness of Christ. Get them so established in the faith until they will not be tossed to and fro and carried about with winds of doctrine. They will all learn how to spell ticdouloureux alike.

All must learn to obey Jesus in everything. "If you love me keep my commandments," said Jesus. This teaching in connection with the spiritual part also will make this vast multitude of one heart and one soul. At first it seems they cared nothing about the doctrine. They got the spiritual blessings and they knew they had the Holy Ghost because they all spake in other tongues as the Spirit gave them utterance.

But we have to admit that the doctrine came to the front later. It is said they continued steadfastly in the apostles' doctrine and fellowship. Then there was the doctrine of circumcision to settle. It was soon decided that the Gentiles should not be required to practice circumcision. There were only four necessary things to carry over to the Gentiles from the Jews. These four necessary things were that they abstain from pollution of idols, and from fornication, and from things strangled, and from blood. These points are still in force today. This is one reason we cannot accept fornicators in the Church now. We must stick to the apostles' doctrine and fellowship along with whatever it takes to make us of one heart and one soul. I do not think the early Church should outdo the Church that is functioning so near the time for the coming of the Lord in being so perfectly joined together in one heart and one soul.

The prayer of Jesus on that memorable night when the Last Supper was instituted was prayed to this end—that we should be of one heart and one soul. I cannot think of Jesus' prayer being lost. That part of it that brings all believers on Jesus into a oneness is especially interesting to me. This is to be the means of getting the message to the balance of the world. It appears that the balance of the world will not be able to believe until the believers are made of one heart and one soul. This certainly puts all believers in a close relationship.

The early Church had it—one heart and one soul. Jesus puts it in His prayer. "That they all may be one," He said, "as thou, Father, art in me, and I in thee." How could there be any closer relation than this? This is like putting a piece of iron in the fire and it stays there till it is white hot, then, it can be said the iron is in the fire and the fire in the iron. Jesus said, "I and my Father are one." Then He prayed that the believers in Jesus shall all be one in that sense. Isn't that wonderful? The iron in the fire and the fire in the iron. Jesus in the believers, and His Father in Him, and by this means all are made perfect in One that the world may not only believe in Jesus but they may know He came from the Father.

How wonderful is such a union! I can understand how the iron is in the fire and the fire in the iron, but I cannot fully comprehend the perfect union of all the believers in Christ on the same principle. But even if I cannot comprehend it I know it is so any way and will come to pass in due time because Jesus prayed the prayer. How could anyone doubt this blessedness materializing when it was the

Almighty Christ praying to His Almighty Father?

I hold myself in readiness to act in my place to bring
this condition to a climax. My soul is jubilant over the out-
look and because I can have a part in such a mighty work.
O Jesus, Thou art wonderful! Thy name is called wonderful. Thy Eternal Father, with whom Thou art so closely
united, will not refuse to grant Thy request. I count it as
already done, and yet it is not done. Multitudes believe in
Thee that do not attempt to obey Thy Word. They are
even against sanctification and the other tongues and will
not practice feet-washing as Thou hast taught us. But they
will come to all of these, won't they? O Jesus, Thou art
worthy to be obeyed. They surely will obey Thee after
awhile. Jesus, I love Thee enough to obey Thee in everything.

As I have thus spoken to my Lord it was in sincerity and
I meant to honor Him by acknowledging His greatness and
the greatness of God. It was Paul that pictured faith as
counting those things that are not as though they are. That
is the way I feel about this oneness that Jesus prayed for.
I know it does not exist now, but it will exist just as sure
as the Bible is true. It will have to come. No power can
prevent it even if it does look impossible. Organizations are
strongly entrenched against the very thing we are working
for. But God in His mighty power can have His way with
me. I will not resist. If He wants to use me and the tens
of thousands who have pledged themselves to stand with
me to break through the lines we are ready for service. We
will not act on presumption, but we will act on the Word
of God.

I rise up in my strength that God gives me and declare
that His Word is true. The iron shall be in the fire and the
fire in the iron! In this sense shall John 17:20-23 be fulfilled. I know it's so. Jesus did not pray that prayer for
nought. He was praying for His disciples when all at once
He said: "Neither pray I for these alone, but for them also
which shall believe on me through their word." Now for
a moment look at the vast multitudes that believe on Jesus as the Christ through the words of the disciples. There

are all the common churches of today besides the Catholics, both Roman and Greek. They all believe on Jesus enough to have set up their forms of worship. By all the forms they have shown that they believe in Jesus. He is the chief One to recognize. Thus they believe in Him. Now this very same multitude that believes in Jesus will come to this oneness—one heart and one soul, in answer to this wonderful prayer. It is so!

When they do this there is only one thing for them to do—drop all of their unnecessary ways and come to the Church of God. They will have to renounce the wrongs and embrace the whole Bible rightly divided which brings them to the apostles' doctrine and fellowship. One heart and one soul is right. I would not know anything about the people of God—all who believe in Jesus through the words of the apostles being joined together in the same mind and in the same judgment—were it not written in our Book. I always feel that I must take the Bible as the Word of God and fully depend upon its teachings. The prayer of Jesus is wonderful. It has been preserved for us. Oh it is wonderful!

"That they all may be one; as thou, Father, art in me, and I in thee, that they also may be one in us: that the world may believe that thou hast sent me. And the glory which thou gavest me I have given them; that they may be one, even as we are one: I in them, and thou in me, that they may be made perfect in one; and that the world may know that thou hast sent me, and hast loved them, as thou hast loved me." (John 17:21-23)

Looking at conditions now, and then looking at the way they will be, see what a contrast there is. It will be a beautiful and pleasant world to live in. The Christians can have no disagreement. There will be no debating, no arguments, no crosses. All will be carried on in unity. The words of all will be smooth words. Words of love. When all of those who believe in Jesus have this love and unity it will be no trouble to reach the other part of the world and convince them that God loves them the same as He loved Jesus. Again I will say this is too wonderful for me, but true as the Bible.

Gigantic Possibilities Are
Within Reach

Searching for the Unseen and Unknown for Use of Mankind

MANY OF THE UNSEEN UNKNOWN BLESSINGS IN GOD'S STOREHOUSE MAY BE OBTAINED IF SOUGHT AFTER

Within the breasts of the people of this generation dormantly lie possibilities, which if not discovered, brought forth and utilized will rob mankind of much good.

Men of science teach and believe that there are great stores of treasures hidden in the earth and sea and sky, for the use of man, undiscovered and undeveloped, and are proving their belief in this by making continuous research. Holes are being drilled in the earth beneath; soundings and search by means of divers and glasses are in constant use in seeking for the discovery of the unknown in the sea.

Men are not only looking at the material within their reach on the surface of the earth and below the surface, but they also have an upward gaze. We are told that powerful guns have been dragged up the mountain sides to the highest peaks and placed with the muzzle upward, heavy charges poured into them, which when discharged, hurled the balls with such velocity that they pierce holes in the sky to an unknown height. Plans have been formulated for attaching wires into these balls with a hope of forming a channel or medium by which something of the unknown could travel like a flash of lightning down to the home of man while the ball was at its greatest height.

For years balloons have been harnessed and loaded with human life, cleaving the sky to a great height, the inmates risking their lives in a little basket hung to a mere canvas loaded with hot air or gas; all with a hope of discovering that which is out of reach of the ordinary walks and attainments of life. In recent years the airships or flying machines are making their way through the upper regions carrying their load of precious freight in the form of human flesh, the intellect of which have ambitions pent up within their own knowledge, with a hope of discovering something of the unknown to harness it for the use and development of man.

As Columbus ventured out from pleasant surroundings into the high seas in search of a shorter passage to the rich spices of India, and instead brought to the knowledge of the inhabitants of the eastern hemisphere the rich country in which we dwell, which has proven to be the best and grandest country of the world, so men are looking downward and upward. They are bounding and plowing through the unknown above with aspirations, no doubt in many cases that are never whispered to the dearest friends lest they should be mocked or met with attempts to discourage.

Astronomers are not idle in their sphere of discovery, but are constantly producing new and more powerful glasses for the purposes of discovering, if possible, new worlds with their inhabitants and peculiar genius that even if there may be no way of communication, their systems, plans or customs might be discovered and brought down to our world for use.

Wireless telegraphy is another factor in the hands of man by which it is hoped that they may be able to so attune their instruments that they will harmonize with and cause to vibrate the cords of a similar instrument operated by the inhabitants of Mars or some of the other planets.

In the physical world men are spending sleepless nights and hazarding their lives with a hope of making some valuable discovery. Men of inventive genius have shut themselves up with no food or companions, while they engaged their mind on some scheme while the train of thought was available, lest a disturbance would cause a disconnection and the whole train of thought be cut asunder and the model in the mind entirely lost before it could become a literal fact that had form and could be observed.

No disturbance is raised; no umbrage is taken against any of the aforesaid ventures, no matter how insane the views and undertakings, but the world looks on with admiration and applause. Even great rewards are offered for new and valued inventions. Thus the physical world is moving on to higher attainments and into a broader sphere of knowledge every year. Pick and shovel, auger and drill, powder and dynamite are brought into use to unearth the unobserved. Diving bells and torpedo boats are assisting men down in the depths of the sea. Balloons and airships are carrying them above in the air, all in search of the unseen and unknown. The physical world is full of excitement, wild prophecies and projects.

Should the spiritual world allow their contemporaries to outwit them? Should the Christian world fold its hands in slumber, sleep long and eat plentifully, and allow the world by going hungry and arising early, to win the prize for energy, with longsuffering, perseverance, grit and determination? Jesus said, "For the children of this world are in their generation wiser than the children of light." But should it be so? With the same untiring effort on the part of the Christian world, many of the unseen and unknown blessings in God's eternal storehouse might be discovered and harnessed for the glory of God, the use of man and for the hastening of the return of our Lord. Latent powers are now lying dormant, unused and unknown in the bosoms and within the reach of many, many today.

Within the grain of wheat is a germ of life, fraught with great possibilities from the sustenance of man by a continual growth and increase as it is placed in the soil, where that germ of life will burst forth into real action. I just feel so with many young lives of today. With proper environments and under certain conditions, those latent powers will spring into use, and not only surprise friends and acquaintances but will in many instances surprise even the persons themselves, because of the successes and exploits wrought.

The grain of wheat, though in it is that germ of life, can lie dormant in the dry granary and finally wither, dry up and blow away as dust. So with men and women in the Christian world today. Men and women love their homes, their friends and companions; and it is almost impossible to get them out of the old family customs and ruts. Like the grain of wheat, although the possibilities and powers for great achievements and exploits for God are in their breasts, yet they can stay at home and follow in the common rote of life, and finally wither away spiritually, dry up and blow away.

Peter and John ran to the sepulchre when they heard that Jesus had disappeared, stooped down and entered in and saw the linen clothes and napkin, but afterward quietly came out and walked away to their own homes, and Mary alone tarried until she saw the vision of angels, and a little later the Lord Himself, and held a conversation with Him.

There are gigantic possibilities within our reach in the vast, illimitable and immeasurable realm of grace, if we will only put forth as much energy and effort to explore and search after them as men do in the physical and scientific world. We are accorded the privilege of looking through a more powerful lens than astronomers have ever invented. We can look, if we close our eyes from the seeing of evil, until we can behold the King in His beauty.

The wireless telegraphy and other wonderful and marvelous inventions of man are only mere specks in comparison to which is attainable by the people of God in this generation. Read the wonderful words of promise: "And to make all men see what is the fellowship (partnership, familiar intercourse) of the mystery, which from the beginning of the world hath been hid in God, who created all things by Jesus Christ: To the intent that now unto the principalities and powers in heavenly places might be known BY THE CHURCH the manifold wisdom of God, According to the eternal purpose which he purposed in Christ Jesus our Lord: In whom we have boldness and access with confidence by the faith of him . . . that ye, being rooted and grounded in love, May be able to comprehend with all saints what is the breadth, and length, and depth, and height; And to know the love of Christ, which passeth knowledge, that ye might be filled with all the fulness of God." (Eph. 3:9-19)

Farewell scientists. Farewell astronomers. Farewell philosophers. Farewell inventive geniuses, explorers and searchers after the unknown; men of worldly wisdom, wit, ambition and grit. "Now unto him that is able to do exceeding abundantly above all that we ask or think, according to the power (latent or unused; germ of life like is in the grain of wheat) that worketh in us, Unto him be glory IN THE CHURCH by Christ Jesus throughout all ages, world without end." (Eph. 3:20, 21)

We should certainly aspire to that high position spoken of and described by Paul, that we might attain to that height in the realm of grace that Christ has obtained for us; that He knows we can reach through Him if we bestir ourselves as He knows we can, and that has been placed within our grasp. "Not as though I had already attained (says Paul), either were already perfect: but I follow after, if that I may apprehend that for which also I am apprehended of Christ Jesus." (Phil. 3:12)

If people would engage themselves in constantly moving on to these higher planes of experience there would be less time for criticism, fault finding, backbiting, caviling over doctrines, and divisions. It is always those who are behind in the race that can see the mistakes, mis-steps and faults of others who are ahead of them. Those who are ahead are so bent on winning the prize that they have no time to look at the faults and mistakes of others, and they are so far ahead in the race that they do not feel the coldness that surrounds the lukewarm and fault-finders in the rear.

This world must be evangelized. "This gospel (power) of the kingdom shall be preached in all the world," in our day. We must not shift this responsibility to a future generation as all other generations have done. There is enough latent power now in men and women, if brought into use, to evangelize the world in five years and usher in the coming of our King. There are possibilities in our young men and young women, and the middle-aged as well, if it were not quenched and locked down by worldly environments, idle matrimony, ungodly and "unequally yoked together" marriages, to fire this world with a fear of God and His power, as Samson's foxes fired the corn fields of the Philistines.

Oh for a million men and women to burst forth, with such holy ambition, with every unused power in full use, like madmen to strike terror and fear to all the half-hearted religionists of the day! John Brown, who with only eighteen men determined to abolish slavery by the seizing of the arsenal at Harper's Ferry, lost his life, but won a place in history because of his boldness and bravery. General Grant rode back and forth on his gallant steed before his great army and cheered and encouraged them on in the battle until the victory was won, although scores and hundreds of his soldiers fell on the field weltering and perishing in their own blood. Should not these daring deeds of reckless bravery put to shame our weak-kneed religious enthusiasm?

Isn't our cause of far greater importance? Shouldn't we be stimulated to the very highest pitch to fight in this most glorious of all battles? Now while we are in the last great conflict can we be satisfied to remain behind where we can see others trudging on in advance, or rushing heedless and reckless into the thickest of the fight? Rouse, ye people! This is the last great conflict. The battle is on! Rush into it to win or die on the field! Look ahead! See the red flag as it waves in the breeze! Behold the enormous possibilities lying unused within your own breast! "PRESS TOWARD THE MARK FOR THE PRIZE OF THE HIGH CALLING OF GOD IN CHRIST JESUS."

The Power of God
Brings Results

This Is The Good News That The Church of God Must Carry Everywhere

THE GOSPEL OF THE KINGDOM NOT WORDS ONLY

Every forward move we make that is in harmony with the Bible is rewarded by outpourings of God's Spirit and power. And we do not consider any move unless it is in harmony with the Bible. We have made several moves that we considered forward moves, and thought we were being led by the unerring Spirit of God, but not until afterward did we learn that they were really forward moves because they were found to be backed up by the Scripture. We are always safe when we have the Holy Spirit and the Holy Scriptures to guide us, and God to set His approval upon us in the way we are going, by sending upon us more demonstrations of His power.

To the Sadducees who were trying to trap Jesus one day He made a statement that is worthy of consideration and much thought. In this statement He very clearly shows the cause of so much error in the world today. That which was true then is certainly true now. Read the way He put it to them that day: "Jesus answered and said unto them, Ye do err, not knowing the scriptures, nor the power of God." (Matt. 22:29)

Now since it is true that those Sadducees erred because they knew not the Scriptures nor the power of God, is it not reasonable to conclude that people in these days will err when they do not know the Scriptures and the power of God? With only this much about the power of God then I conclude I am on safe footing when I make the statement that the power of God brings results. And this one incident in the life of Jesus was of such great importance that it was mentioned by two of the writers, but given in a little different manner. Now read it from the other writer: "And Jesus answering said unto them, Do ye not therefore err, because ye know not the scriptures, neither the power of God?" (Mark 21:24)

We very readily conclude that the Scriptures are indispensible. Jesus linked the Scriptures and the power together in this wonderful statement. To carry on right, then I conclude that they are inseparable. We must have the Bible and power of God. The Bible is a book that can be read and handled, but the power cannot be seen or handled, but it can be felt. And our bodies can quiver and shake under the power of God as the leaf shakes and quivers when the wind blows upon it. The wind cannot be seen but it can be felt, and the effects of its power or movements can be seen.

By this time I think all that are following this message can see that it takes the Bible and the power to keep us out of error. And the power of God is always in harmony with the Bible and the Bible is always in agreement with the power of God. Error in connection with the Bible comes from wrong interpretations or opinions of men. And when there is no manifestation of power to accompany these interpretations people should be wise and frank enough to drop their opinions. Now isn't this the sensible way of looking at it? If we do not witness the demonstrations of power among our people it would give cause for concern and fear. But seeing and knowing of the power of God falling gives cause for confidence and much rejoicing. Every since 1908 when the Lord baptized me with the Holy Ghost and fire I have noticed it has become common among our people to speak about the power falling. Some times the power would fall upon only a few so they would dance, leap, shout, talk in tongues, handle serpents and fire, and other times it would fall upon scores and even hundreds in the large congregations. And I am not sure that I have not witnessed a thousand at one time demonstrating under the influence of the power of God similar to the thousands of leaves fluttering under the power of the wind. And to this agrees the apostle Paul when he says, "Now there are diversities of gifts, but the same Spirit. And there are differences of administrations, but the same Lord. And there are diversities of operations, but it is the same God which worketh all in all. But the manifestation of the Spirit is given to every man to profit withal." (1 Cor. 21:4-7)

Some people are against the power of God like they are against cyclones and tornadoes. When the power begins to fall there is usually a cry raised about fanaticism and wild fire. But we have what people call "freak winds" that amaze people and cause them to wonder. But they do not cry fanaticism or wild fire at the wind. Then why may we not have some "freak" manifestations of the power of God occasionally without getting frightened for fear someone is becoming fanatical? Indeed we may, and we are going to have them more and more as we keep on going the way that pleases God. Paul says "diversities of operations," and diversities mean different and a variety of them. The Lord does not want us to go along in one rut all the time so He has arranged for the power to waft and whip us about in different ways occasionally to have variety. And our people especially have no right to cry fanaticism or wild fire or get scared when something different suddenly makes its appearance among us when the power is falling. To such people that sit back and criticize when the power is falling and people are demonstrating, I would say that they had better get under the shower themselves and then they will see nothing to criticize. And wouldn't Jesus say to such critics both in the Church and outside, "Ye do err, not knowing the scriptures, nor the power of God"?

Paul laid special emphasis upon the power of God in his writings. When he found the Corinthian church crossed up and with divisions among them he told them he would not judge between the right and the wrong by their words in testimony or conversation but he would judge by the power. Those that had no power would be considered in fault and those upon whom the power was operating would be considered in the right. Read what he says, "But I will

come to you shortly, if the Lord will, and will know, not
the speech of them which are puffed up, but the power.
For the kingdom of God is not in word, but in power."
(1 Cor. 4:19, 20)

This is Paul emphasizing the value of the power, and encouraging the saints to be sure they are in such favor with
God that the power will operate them. This same truth
is verified by other writings among which are words as follows: "And I, brethren, when I came to you, came not with
excellency of speech or of wisdom, declaring unto you the
testimony of God. For I determined not to know any thing
among you, save Jesus Christ, and him crucified. And I was
with you in weakness, and in fear, and in much trembling.
And my speech and my preaching was not with enticing
words of man's wisdom, but in demonstration of the Spirit
and of power: That your faith should not stand in the wisdom of men, but in the power of God." (1 Cor. 2:1-5)

And Paul gave all of this explanation in order to attract
from mere words to the power of God. Please remember
that Jesus teaches that people err when they do not know
the Scriptures or the power of God. And is it any wonder
that there is so much error in the world when people stick
so firmly to their forms of godliness and deny or rule out
the power of God? And we are told to stay away from
people who deny the power. They are dangerous because
they are already in error. And those who remain with
them will also fall into error. Those who deny the power
are classed with blasphemers, trucebreakers, despisers of those
that are good, traitors and lovers of pleasure more than
lovers of God. All of these and still they have a form of
godliness. (2 Tim. 3:2-5)

It is my desire to encourage our people to be in possession
of this power of God wherever they go. I believe they
know this but I want to emphasize the importance of having our faith in the power. I conclude the power is of
more real importance than eloquent sermons and discourses.
I am sure it is of more value than any sermons or discourses without the power. I do not consider that mere
sermons or discourses without the power can be the gos-

pel. It is the power that is the gospel in reality and the sermons are only the filling. I am not disparaging the value of preaching, but preaching with no power is a waste of time and energy. Without the power of God the preacher is liable to preach error instead of the truth. It takes the power to keep the preacher out of error. Is that putting it too strong? Well, Jesus said, "Ye do err, not knowing the scriptures, nor the power of God." I am trying to show the importance of being so humble and consecrated while preaching that the power of God will be present to bring results. And it is the power of God that brings results. And this is the good news that the Church of God must carry everywhere.

Paul proved that he was in favor of the power and stated that he was not ashamed of it. He demonstrated under the power of God in preference to delivering eloquent discourses. He said this was for the purpose of getting the faith of his audience in the power rather than in the wisdom of men. And he seemed a little surprised that the Corinthians converts had fallen into error after he had endeavored to have them put their faith in the power instead of in words. But they were switched off to words and formed their different opinions. This brought division. The power has the effect of bringing unity, while men's opinions put in words bring division. Then let us cling to the power that brings results, and acknowledge that the power of God is the gospel that must be carried into all the world. The apostle Paul said, ". . . I am not ashamed of the gospel of Christ: for it is the power of God unto salvation to every one that believeth . . ." (Rom. 1:16)

I have been told that the gospel is the story of Jesus being the Saviour of the world and the words of the story is the power. But I rather conclude that the gospel is the power rather than the words. That is, "it," "the gospel," is the power. That is, the power of God is the gospel. And this view is emphasized when we consider other verses given by the same writer. Now read carefully with this thought in mind: "Not that we are sufficient of ourselves to think any thing as of ourselves; but our sufficiency is of God; Who also hath made us able ministers of the new testament;

not of the letter, (not mere words), but of the spirit (the power of God): for the letter (mere words) killeth, but the spirit giveth life." (2 Cor. 3:4, 6)

He was made an able minister but not that kind that produced mere words that kill, but that kind that demonstrates by the Spirit and the power of God so that our faith should stand in the power of God of which he was not ashamed. And this power brought results. Now read again from this demonstrator: "For I will not dare to speak of any of those things which Christ hath not wrought by me, to make the Gentiles obedient, by word and deed, Through mighty signs and wonders, by the power of the Spirit of God; so that from Jerusalem, and round about unto Illyricum, I have fully preached the gospel of Christ." (Rom. 14:18, 19)

These verses plainly state that it takes the power to fully preach the gospel. So then Paul could have said that he was not ashamed of the power of God. And we all know it takes the power to save, and it takes the power to sanctify. Merely convincing people by argument does not save them. No, it takes the power of God to bring results. And the gospel of the kingdom is not words only, but the power of God. This is voiced by the Scriptures also. Read, "For the kingdom of God is not in word, but in power." (1 Cor. 4:20) "For our gospel came not unto you in word only, but also in power . . ." (1 Thess. 1:5)

We understand that God pours out His power upon His children who are walking humbly and obediently before Him. In other words He gives us showers of His power when we are going in the way that pleases Him. Then taking the Church as a whole we are surely doing things that please Him. Reports of revivals are coming into this office by the scores and hundreds. I think I never heard of so many sweeping revivals. Multitudes are coming to the Lord. The power falls in nearly every service—at the regular meetings as well as in the protracted meetings. I do not hear of great preaching so much but more mention is made of the falling of the power. I am made to exclaim in the language of the prophet as he prophesied of us and this time: "Thou shalt arise, and have mercy upon Zion: for the time to favour her, yea, the set time, is come." (Psa. 102:13)

When Will Jesus Come?

When the Work Is Done and the Church Is Ready to Receive Him

WE ARE NOW IN THE PREPARATION TIME

"My little finger shall be thicker than my father's loins." This was a statement that the young men of the kingdom of Israel advised the fourth king of Israel to make when he was taking the throne of his father, Solomon. On account of this statement and the meaning of it given, he suddenly lost the good will of a large number of his subjects. The ten tribes revolted and pulled away under the leadership of Jeroboam and instituted what was afterward designated Israel, or the northern kingdom. This revolt was according to prophecy. That is, one of the prophets had prophesied that Jeroboam should have ten tribes after Solomon's death and only two tribes should remain in the house of David under Rehoboam. In order to have this prophecy fulfilled it was put in the mouth of Rehoboam to answer Israel roughly and say, "And now whereas my father did lade you with a heavy yoke, I will add to your yoke: my father hath chastised you with whips, but I will chastise you with scorpions." (1 Kings 12:11)

Thus every prophecy of our good Book must be fulfilled. With only a hasty but accurate inspection of this Book compared with history it will be readily seen that every prophecy that has been due for fulfillment in the past has been fulfilled to the letter. There was no force or combination of events or happenings that ever prevented their fulfillment. But rather, on the other hand, there were always combinations of events, though sometimes very odd, similar to the few words spoken by Rehoboam. That was an odd expression—a very small pivot upon which to turn a whole nation—"My little finger shall be thicker than my father's loins," but it turned that whole nation as soon as spoken and forced that vast multitude into two nations in a very few minutes. All the prophecies that are due for fulfillment in the future are just as sure.

Unfailing prophecies show that the Church of the last days shall prosper and be in health. The world shall be subjugated to our Christ. It shall be informed of our coming. The nations shall become weak and submissive. Resistance shall be taken away from them and all shall walk under one government just as truly as the wild animals of the forest became tame and docile when the time was ripe for their entering into Noah's new ship. I do not know what odd statements may be made to bring about some of the changes that are destined to take place, but something will happen to change the minds of millions in a minute. God works quickly sometimes, as in the case of Rehoboam, while at other times it has been truly said, "God's mill grinds slow but sure." It is stated that God is going to make a short work in the last days. And by His saving, a short work, I conclude it will have to be a quick work, because we have such a long distance to go, as we count distance, to get the work finished. The work must be finished. Yes, it just has to be finished.

We want the Lord to return. We think He is the only hope for this world of confusion and distress; thus we want Him to come back and set everything right and in perfect harmony. We look for the fulfillment of the statement made by the angels when they sang, "On earth peace, good will toward men." It has been anything else but peaceful ever since that vast multitude sang that wonderful chorus. But still we cannot think of anything else because of the meaning of those wonderful words, and the many prophecies and statements contained in our Book besides.

But when is this mighty Christ of the Bible going to return? People have been looking for Him day and night for many years. But He has not come yet. We have been taught to look for Him any moment. We have often said, "He may come tonight." But still He has not returned. The early Church looked for His soon coming. They became so enthused about it that Paul had to set them right to keep them from teaching falsely. He indicated that some had already commenced to teach that He would soon be back. I take this view because he called on the early Church to beware of deceivers. He said about this very subject, "Let no man deceive you." Let us read the verses and get the import.

"Now we beseech you, brethren, by the coming of our Lord Jesus Christ, and by our gathering together unto him, That ye be not soon shaken in mind, or be troubled, neither by spirit, nor by word, nor by letter as from us, as that the day of Christ is at hand. Let no man deceive you by any means: for that day shall not come, except there come a falling away first." (2 Thess. 2:1-3)

Thus Paul plainly told the brethren that they need not look for Jesus to return until after the great falling away period which did take place later according to history. So now we are on this side of the great apostasy which led into which is known in history as dark ages. And we have a better right to look for Him now than they did then. But Paul was afraid they would be deceived about it and he did not want them deceived. It has been many centuries since the great apostasy and still He has not come, but He will come yet. And He says He will come quickly when He does come. (Rev. 22:7)

But when will He come? Men have set the time. They have claimed the Lord revealed to them the time. Others have counted the years and spent months and even years in making their calculation, trying to work it out that way, but all have failed. He has not come yet. But I say, when will He come? As stated above we have been taught to look for Him every day. And we have looked faithfully and still He has not come. We have been taught that He would slip in on us unawares as a thief in the night. And He has not come that way. They used to tell us that probably mother would be taken and father and children left, because mother was good enough and they would be left to go through the tribulation period. It has been announced through religious papers that a certain good man had disappeared and it was believed the Lord had slipped him away without dying. But that never happened. With all the different theories advanced, and all the opinions expressed, with people sometimes dressing themselves in white robes and going out to meet Him on a certain day, still He has never yet come. Many have been deceived in later years as well as when Paul wrote to the early Church that warning. Jesus has not yet returned, but we know He will come at the appointed time.

But when will He come? Many know but little more than is contained on the surface of the text I have used at the conventions for years. "Therefore be ye also ready: for in such an hour as ye think not the Son of man cometh." (Matt. 24:44) I have been insisting that we hasten to get ready since we are not ready. This we are doing. We are working hard because now is the time of preparation. The preparation time is marked out by the prophecy concerning the running of automobiles. I think most of our people see now that it is not only a good spiritual experience that is required to make us ready, but also that certain work must be done before we are ready. And that work is not yet done. So we are hurrying on as fast as we can to get ready—that is, to get the work done that is plainly pointed out by the prophecies and Jesus Himself.

Jesus will come and we are still looking forward to His coming, but in connection with this we are expecting to get the work done that we know is required. We do not want our people deceived any more than Paul ever wanted his people deceived. But we still know He is coming. And this in connection with the resurrection that is set for about the same time, is our hope. But when, oh when will He come? We do not seem to be so much concerned about the exact time of His coming, since we have learned that certain work has to be done in order to fulfill prophecy. This prophecy requires the Church to be perfected so He can present it to Himself a glorious Church not having spot or wrinkle or any such thing. Then we have discovered that Jesus is not going to make us ready, but that we have to make ourselves ready. This is shown by a number of Scriptures that cannot fail. (Eph. 4:11-16; 1 John 3:2, 3; Rev. 19:7) Making ourselves like Him. He finished the work He had to do. We must finish the work that is required of us. And that is, getting the Church ready and getting it filled, like Noah finished his big ship and got it filled before the flood came. I do not want our people deceived concerning this subject.

Still I ask earnestly and boldly, when is Jesus coming so it can be said, "On earth peace, good will toward men"? Or does this mean He had to be here in person when this happens, or is He going to act as the Head of the Church while He still sits at the right hand of God and directs the work of subjugation in a similar manner to that of a general of an army who sits in his headquarters office and directs the battle? On account of certain Scriptures it would seem that the latter view is rather to be favored. Then if this is the case the heavier the responsibilities are that fall upon us. And this is what I have been trying to impress upon our people for years. Now notice a few verses in connection with this subject. When Peter was preaching that second memorable sermon that brought in the five thousand he made the following statement that never has been changed but is rather verified by the holy prophets:

"And he shall send Jesus Christ, which before was preached unto you: Whom the heaven must receive until the times of restitution of all things, which God hath spoken by the mouth of all his holy prophets since the world began." (Acts 3:20, 21)

The Syriac version verifies the King James version and assists in making it plainer. Read the same verses from this version:

"And times of rest may come to you from the face of the Lord; and he may send to you him, who was made ready for you, Jesus the Messiah: Whom the heavens must retain, until the completion of the times of those things, which God hath spoken by the mouth of his holy prophets of old." (Acts 3:20, 21)

The authorized version says concerning Jesus, "Whom the heaven must receive until" the same certain time.

In that first wonderful message after he was baptized with the Holy Ghost, and the one that landed three thousand souls, Peter made the statement that Jesus should remain at the right hand of the Father until His foes are made His footstool. The writer of Hebrews also makes a similar statement as he tells of Jesus who sat down on the right hand of God to remain there "expecting till his enemies be made his footstool."

When is our Lord coming back to earth? I do not know when He is coming, but it is evident that the time is set and when that time comes He will come and not tarry. It is evident also that He is not going to come and slip away a few without anybody knowing anything about it. How could it be that way in the face of Paul's declaration of what is going to happen then? Some noise and some miraculous happening. Somebody may think that will be no exciting time, but when all that takes place that Paul tells of I would not think of it being anything else but thrilling and exciting. It is already exciting to me while I am trying to make ready for the greatest reception that ever has been recorded on the pages of history. Now read what Paul says:

"Then we which are alive and remain shall be caught up together with them in the clouds, to meet the Lord in the air: and so shall we ever be with the Lord." (1 Thess. 4:17)

This is in the future, but I want you to understand what is to be done yet to fulfill prophecy and make fully ready for this glorious event. And it is evident that we have to do our work while He is retained in heaven. And the work to fulfill prophecy will bring in the multitudes, teach them the all things, make them perfect and presentable so He can justly be proud of them and all of us. In other words, to be ready for the coming of the Lord is having certain things accomplished that fulfill prophecy. And since the time set for His coming is now so near at hand we must do our work rapidly. There is no time for idleness. This is the way I feel about it, and I believe my feelings are prompted by the same Spirit that prompted the prophets.

While I am trying to hurry the work along by my statements and letters, I do not want my fellow-laborers to think of my being like Rehoboam promised his subjects. I do not want to be too hard on any of the workers, but I do want them to work. I can't bear for a pastor to just merely be a preacher on Sunday and let the wolves harass and carry off the sheep all the week while he is lying around idle and contented to do so. I am getting nearer and nearer to the point where I think the pastor should put in full hours, in rounding up his sheep and protecting his lambs, the same as the man that works in the mill to earn money upon which to pay tithes to support the shepherd. The evangelists too, while "all around them souls are dying," do nothing sometimes because they say they have no opening or no money to pay their transportation to some far-away field. There are always people near by that will die and lose their souls without somebody makes some extra effort in prayer and sometimes pushing the message upon them even when they do not want it.

I know Jesus is coming soon. I know the multitudes must be reached and saved. I can't be easy and restful about the work. I feel that I must work. I feel that my fellow-ministers must work. And when they do not, then I wonder if they have ever caught the vision as they should. It is to such as these I want to say, "More is in you, put it in operation for the Church of God." If we do have those with us who are not capable of finding a place to work or cannot work without being told by the foreman or chief engineer, then I think it is time for us to enlarge our organization so everyone can have the necessary assistance to keep them all busy. In the last days they are to be commanded to go out quickly and bring them in, and go out into the highways and hedges and compel them to come in that the Church may be filled to fulfill prophecy.

Our God Must Be Reverenced

His Word Shall Be Fulfilled And The Multitudes Gathered Into The Church

Who wants to challenge God? Who wants to stand out in defiance of His Holy Bible? Too many have undertaken this already. They have been ingloriously defeated. Their bones are moldering in the grave while the Book itself and the God of the Bible still live on. Who would be so unwise as to speak things they do not know, and undertake to trifle, or meddle, or interfere, with God's infallible and unfailing program? Those who would undertake to do so are nothing more than gnats in the hands of His almighty Sovereignty.

When only a small boy, a deep impression was made on my mind, when my father told of a man who had sent out a challenge to God. In loud boastful language he declared there was no God. He defied His appearance and cursed His name. The man was fearless and boastful. He was thrown into a dreadful rage when anyone would speak of God with holy reverence and fear in his presence. He made such ado about it that the whole country round about became interested and almost excited. People became aroused for miles around because of his wild and boastful expressions. At times he acted almost like a madman. In fact, he was mad against God and took a delight in letting it be known.

It seemed that he deliberately decided to put God to the test, and undertake to prove to the God-fearing public that there was no God. He announced a day and place where he was going to publicly and fearlessly challenge God. He constructed a high platform and made all of the necessary preparations. The day came and the people came by the thousands. The hour came and he walked proudly up on the platform. His blasphemous words of defiance were so vile that the people almost recoiled and retreated. It was only a few minutes until he struck the fatal blow as he challenged

God, "If there is a God, strike me down," he said, and if that was not done it would prove there is no God.

Scarcely had he finished his last sentence when a little insect smaller than a gnat rested on the side of his neck. Instantly he fell in a heap upon the floor of that platform. That was the last of him and his blasphemous words of defiance against God. And the people felt a sense of relief and retained their same God-fearing spirit, and showed even more reverence for the God of the Bible.

This was a little like Elijah's experience on Mount Carmel with the four hundred and fifty prophets of Baal. There came a time when something had to be done to save Israel from the Baal worship. Elijah was God's man to do it. He was only one lone prophet of the Lord while Baal's prophets were four hundred and fifty. The multitudes were gathered together when Elijah walked confidently before them. "How long halt ye between two opinions?" came through the vocal organs of that man of God. "If the LORD be God, follow him: but if Baal, then follow him." (1 Kings 18:21) This was such a strange challenge that the people were speechless. But he did not stop there. He had gone too far to stop. As God's representative and prophet he must vindicate God. The final test was made when Baal's prophets called in vain until after midday for their god to answer by fire. But no fire came. Then it was Elijah's time. When he called upon his God—our God—the fire "fell and consumed the burnt sacrifice, and the wood, and the stones, and the dust, and licked up the water that was in the trench." And when the people saw it, they fell on their faces and began to cry out, "The LORD, he is the God; the LORD, he is the God."

In the time of the early Church there were some startling happenings that drove the people to God and put them in fear. When it was discovered by Peter, that mighty apostle, that Ananias and Sapphira his wife, had lied to God, and they both had fallen down at his feet, great fear came upon all the Church and as many as heard these things. While this fear prevailed there was a wholesale rush to the God of the Apostles. The record states that multitudes, both of men and women were added to the Lord. Indeed, God is

God, and He is the mighty God. He is the same mighty God that He has been in other ages. The words in His Book have the same weight as in days of old. It may be that we are nearing the time for the fulfillment of prophecy when the Lord is going to do some more of His strange work and bring to pass some more of His strange acts. He has done wonders in the past and will do more wonders as time moves on. In fact, His program must and will be carried out.

No one need be incredulous or sceptical about getting the work done that must be done before Jesus comes. The every creature message must go to the every creature. All nations must be taught. Just as truly must all nations be baptized in the name of the Father, and of the Son and of the Holy Ghost. After this is done, they are to be taught to observe all things that Jesus commanded His disciples. What is the use for this to be doubted? His words were spoken with power (Luke 4:32), and they have lost none of their original force. Others have doubted, but we must not. And according to these words it is not enough to merely tell the all nations and let them believe and accept the Lord's doctrine if they want to, and if they don't they can turn it down. But to obey the Lord we are under just as much obligation to baptize them and teach them to observe the all things as we are to merely give them the gospel. We are to open their eyes and turn them from darkness to light, and from the power of Satan to God. We must make them see. It is not a question as to whether they want to see or not, they must be made to see. No matter about the difficulties of such a task, it just has to be done. Isn't God, God? Isn't He back of His Word? Could any force prevent Elijah's proving to that sceptical mass of people that God was God? No, the fire fell in spite of all their unbelief and the four hundred and fifty Baal prophets that had shouted themselves hoarse trying to get their god to comply with their request. Just as well expect God's fire to fall now right in the presence of atheists, infidels and sceptical people.

I tell you, my beloved fellow-laborers for God and His truth, I believe what Jesus says about the every creature message, and the all nations activities. I absolutely refuse to limit the power of the Holy One. That is just what the children of Israel did when Moses was leading them from Egypt to Canaan. We are warned against doing the thing that caused them to fail in the wilderness. I am going to believe God and His Word. You are going to do the same thing. In Moses' time the unbelievers and idolaters were destroyed under the wrath of God, but now, in these days, God is working differently. A few may be slain like Ananias and Sapphira were, but the masses are going to be walked into the Church of God in a similar manner to the way God walked the animals into Noah's new ship. I tell you, they had to come. And God has just as much power over men as He had to convert wild, ferocious, bloodthirsty beasts into docile creatures so they could go into the ark. They could not go into the ark until they were saved from their fighting disposition and blood-thirstiness. And we are not supposed to take people into the Church till they are saved and promise to go on into all the Bible teaches. And they are not supposed to be always about getting sanctified and baptized with the Holy Ghost and fire.

When the multitudes get into the Church, then comes the time for perfecting the Church. This, then, is the work of the ministers. "For the perfecting of the saints," says Paul. And these saints are to be made up of the "all nations" that are to be baptized.

"Till we all come in the unity of the faith, and of the knowledge of the Son of God, unto a perfect man, unto this measure of the stature of the fulness of Christ." (Eph. 4:13)

Now I would have you to understand that this mass of human flesh is not going to be just a few as some would try to have us believe, but rather the all nations. Agreeable to this statement is Paul as he visions the finishing up time of the last days, "Warning every man." Where is any left out? "And teaching every man." Again I say, where is any left out? You know this is true. I am not alone. But traditions would have us limit this perfected mass of people to only a few. But we must break away from traditions and embrace and cling to the Bible as it is for us today in this great and mighty last days movement. The few would do for the past, but nothing short of multitudes are marked out for us today. "They shall not be few" says the prophet. And this refers to those who are to be glorified. "I will also glorify them, and they shall not be small." Who is He going to glorify? That mass of people that shall not be few and shall not be small. Paul says, "that we may present every man perfect." He also says, "That he might present it to himself a glorious church, not having spot, or wrinkle, or any such thing; but that it should be holy and without blemish." (Eph. 5:27) And we all know this is the Church of the Bible. This is the only institution that we know of that is to be glorified.

Our work then is made clear. Our duty is plainly seen. Gathering into the Church the multitudes instead of only a few. All nations instead of a few from all nations. No wonder the missionary zeal is eating us up. No wonder the states have been having the spirit of friendly rivalry in trying to raise the most money. And when this spirit, like a garment, is thrown over the people they give of their means when they don't want to and when they do not aim to. Some have acknowledged that very thing to me. This is like God getting into the legs of those wild beasts of the forest and walking them into Noah's new ship that had never before been loaded with a cargo. Neither has the Church ever been filled, but it WILL BE FILLED, and the last method to be employed to finish filling it will be the compelling method. This principle was shown by the cows that were yoked up to the new cart loaded with the "ark of the covenant," taking it back to its rightful owners. The cows did not want to go and leave their calves and their home. But they went anyhow. They had to go, God got in their legs and made them go, just like He got into Mr. and Mrs. Lion and Mr. and Mrs. Giraffe and made them go into that big ship that had to be filled. To show that the cows did not want to go, the record states that they "went along the highway, lowing as they went." This is the work of our God. And HE IS OUR GOD.

I wonder if we may have some doubters and incredulous ministers in our ranks who are helping us pull the load and yet they grumble as they pull. I wonder if God makes them help us when they prefer not to. I wonder if they low like the cows and still help us pull the Church and its work along. They may not like the W. M. B. and say—"money, money, money, everything is money." Still they pull and keep right on the highway that leads to the goal. The cows took the ark to the big harvest field of Joshua before they stopped, even if they did low and grumble and long to be back at home with their calves. Some of these grumblers, if there should be any, are making a bee line for the big harvest field where the golden grain must be reaped. Thank the Lord for the helpers whether they want to help or not. God make them help. They have to help or they wouldn't. Just this year a man called me and gave me money for our missionary work and grumbled as he gave it. I held out my hand and smiled while he grumbled and pulled the money out of his wallet. As he handed me the money, I had a spell and thanked him for it while he looked glum and sour. I knew the Lord made him do it. But he was buying souls and by and by he will get his reward when he sees the souls his money purchased. His grumbling will cease when he gets his eyes fully open so he can see the blessedness of service, and full recognize the power of God, and the great work for which we are responsible. With Jesus, let us altogether say, "My Father worketh hitherto, and I work." (John 5:17) "I must work the works of him that sent me, while it is day: the night cometh, when no man can work." (John 9:4) And I shall never expect to be satisfied until I have the assurance and evidence that every member in the Church of God is a worker.

Hold Fast to the Right

The Early Church Thrived On Persecution And Hardship

WARRIORS OF THE LAST DAYS NEED KNOW NO DEFEAT

In the early days of the Church of God many of the members were literally driven from their homes by the severe persecutions that swept the city of Jerusalem. They were scattered abroad over the regions round about. Those were indeed stormy days for the new beginners of this great institution. They were untrained, without knowledge and good understanding of the general workings of the new institution as intended by its Founder. About all they knew was a spiritual experience—they were baptized with the Holy Ghost and fire. Imagine the hardships, difficulties, roamings and sufferings of those early saints. Probably the first night out they were without shelter or food. The second and third nights were no better, with the children tired, the mothers worn, footsore and weary, and the men anxious and wondering what to do.

Men and women were surprised in their homes and were rushed off to prison. Hard-hearted men in authority snatched mothers from their children, slapped down the little boys and girls that were clinging to mother's clothing, and rushed the mother off to prison, leaving a house full of helpless ones crying, screaming and frightened so badly they almost went into spasms—left to die of starvation and exposure. General destruction of the Church lay in the wake of these cruel marauders. Those heartless devastators were determined to crush the life out of the b a b y organization, before its members had time to steady themselves and become established and able to meet oppositions.

Amidst all these tremendous storms of persecutions that broke in upon the Church it is not known that even one member weakened and turned traitor and renounced his faith and turned back the other way. They could be landed in prison, separated from their families, driven from their homes, mocked and accused, threatened and whipped, but they could not be frightened into abandoning the cause they had espoused. And, besides this, those that escaped the prisons went everywhere and spread the good news of salvation through Jesus Christ, who had been so cruelly treated and put to death a short while before. Every move that was made to destroy the Church of God only became a means of strengthening it. Thus it grew and the members were multiplied until they were numbered by the multitudes. It was but a little while until the baby institution was transformed into a stalwart giant.

The mighty acts of the early membership of the Church of God, as left on record for our perusal, were accomplished because the grace of God was so powerful that it transformed prison floors into beds of roses, scourges and lashes into streamers of velvet, grim prison walls into forts to ward off the missiles of Satan, and stocks into joyful religious services, prison cells into pulpits and midnight earthquakes into altar calls that made salvation flow like an overflowing stream. Everything that undertook to frighten and destroy brought a flood of rejoicing and glad hallelujahs. The lives of those early Church members were so marvelously and wonderfully transformed by the power of Jesus Christ that nothing could frighten or induce them to give up their precious faith and experience.

We are without knowledge of what we may have to endure, or in what way we will be called upon to glorify God. But since those early-day saints and members of the Church were given grace to hold on faithfully under such adversities, surely grace for our emergencies will be provided. The tremendous attacks of Satan and his hosts came upon these early heroes so suddenly, and even before they had had time for training or warning, and still they remained true as steel. We have the records of those early days, and many of us have had years of experience.

The Lord is wonderfully holding the persecutions in check so they have not broken down upon us suddenly. God is giving us time to prepare ourselves by forcing a more gradual approach. So it would seem unnecessary for us to falter and quail under the more gradual attacks. If we can't bear the more gradual approach of whatever seems inevitable, then we will prove ourselves insufficient and unqualified and unworthy of the honor conferred upon us as eleventh-hour laborers and last-days Church of God warriors.

I have no fears of cowardice being displayed. I believe I am surrounded with a large group of braves who are ready and prepared and well equipped for the fray, no matter how suddenly it may break over the ramparts and rush in upon us. Many of these braves are here today who have already boldly and fearlessly declared "you can count on me."

This company of heroic loyalists is not only composed of men, but also of women. Loyal blood is coursing through their veins, and they are so established in the Church of God that no intimidation or power of any foe can induce them to draw back or give up. In fact, I feel that I can speak for these noble men and women in terms of the highest praise, and display the utmost confidence in them by saying on their behalf that there is not in them the least disposition to retreat or surrender. With us here, it is hold on to and go on with the Church of God, as marked out in New Testament Scriptures as long as breath is in our bodies and heart beats continue.

The World is Ours
Thru Christ

Move Forward With Speed to Accomplish the Work

THE HOUSE MUST BE FILLED

Perhaps it would not be wrong to turn this around and say that the world is to be Christ's by us. That is, by our work and service as instruments through which the Holy Ghost may work in harmony with the Scriptures. Since the Holy Spirit moved the prophets to speak the words in the first place, why not the same Holy Spirit move us to produce the things prophesied? For instance, the Holy Spirit prompted Paul to write, "All things are yours," then where are the people that are going to give the same Holy Spirit the chance to work through them till Paul's statement is fully realized? Then as another example, the sweet singer of Israel spake as he was moved by the Holy Ghost when he marked out or surveyed out our possessions. And these possessions are to be ours for the asking.

"Ask of me, and I shall give thee the heathen for thine inheritance, and the uttermost parts of the earth for thy possession." (Psa. 2:8)

Since the Holy Spirit moved upon David to deliver that message, then why should it be thought a thing incredible for the same Holy Spirit to move upon His own chosen people to utter the prayers and then move right out and begin to take possession?

Listen at Paul again as he spake as the Holy Spirit moved upon him. And surely no one will think of raising any question with Paul. "Therefore let no man glory in men. For all things are yours; Whether Paul, or Apollos, or Cephas, or the world, or life, or death, or things present, or things to come; all are yours; And ye are Christ's; and Christ is God's." (1 Cor. 3:21-23)

Where is the limit? Even Paul acknowledged that he, himself, was to be owned and possessed by that favored host to which is given the all things and the might that cannot be resisted when the time comes. This would call for a statement from Hebrews which shows that all of the good and mighty men of faith would still be imperfect without this mighty host filled with the Holy Ghost pointed out by prophecy to subdue the world and take possession of it. You know it is declared by the writer of Hebrews who spake as he was moved by the Holy Ghost that the mighty men catalogued in the eleventh chapter all died out but did not receive the promises, but only saw them afar off.

"These all died in faith, not having received the promises, but having seen them afar off, and were persuaded of them, and embraced them, and confessed that they were strangers and pilgrims on the earth." (Heb. 11:13)

They confessed this, and accepted their fate with patience, but they saw a time coming when the certain chosen people would get such unqualified and unrestricted control of the world that they will not have to be strangers and pilgrims on the earth as they were.

"And these all, having obtained a good report through faith, received not the promise: God having provided some better thing for us, that they without us should not be made perfect."

Who is the host that will be accounted the US? It is certainly not Paul, because he declared he was owned and possessed by the mass that was to subdue and possess the world. It has not been any body of people in the past. It has to be a people living now or near in the future. It has to be men of faith and some powerful works as well. It has to be a people who will have favor with all the people of the world that will be subdued. This subjugation will not be wrought by bloody war material such as subdued Ethiopia in 1936, and such as has been used in all bloody conquests to acquire territory and parts of the world. But this great government will take possession so it can be said there was not a gun fired, like it was said that Solomon's Temple, which is a type, went up without the sound of a hammer.

Please do not think of me being beside myself, when I bring to your minds things you already know. I have carried you almost nowhere yet to compare with where the Church of God is going to carry you a little later on. In the past we have been feeling along as if we were afraid the ice would break, looking for Jesus to come every day or every night because we had been trained in that way. A story is told of a man traveling in the northwest during a severe cold spell. He came to a river that was frozen over. He walked up carefully to the edge, tried the ice to see if it would bear his weight. He was so fearful that it would not hold up under him that he got down on his knees and reached forward with his hands to try the ice ahead of his weight. He had not gone more than twenty or thirty feet until he heard a big noise of horses hoofs behind him. He looked around and there came a sled loaded with bog iron and the horses in a trot right on the very same ice he had been so fearful of. He rose up on his feet and watched that team with the load as they trotted briskly past him. He was so amazed that he could not move. After the team came out on the other side he decided to walk on instead of crawl.

Thank God the prophecies will not smash under us. Let us move forward at a rapid rate of speed to make ready for the return of the Lord. But this is not saying we are looking for Him tonight. But it is saying that there is certain work to be done, and we know what it is, and there is so much of it that we know we have to hurry to get it done in time, so we can comply with the words of Jesus when He said, "Therefore be ye also ready: for in such an hour as ye think not the Son of man cometh." (Matt. 24:44) It is a fact that somebody must and will be ready. His Church will be ready. We are not laboring in vain when we toil day and night to get souls to perfect and make ready. Paul states that he was a minister of the same Church that is going to succeed in gathering the multitudes in and getting them ready for presentation. Paul had just made mention of suffering in his flesh for the sake of the Church, then he adds: "Whereof I am made a minister, according to the dispensation of God which is given to me for you, to fulfil the word of God; Even the mystery which hath been hid from ages and from generations, but now is made manifest to his saints: To whom God would make known what is the riches of the glory of this mystery among the Gentiles; which is Christ in you, the hope of glory: Whom we preach, warning every man (EVERY MAN) and teaching every man in all wisdom; that we may present every man (EVERY MAN) perfect in Christ Jesus." (Col. 1:25-28)

It is not enough to hunt up every man and warn him, but teaching every man, goes with it. And not merely teach him till he rises to the fifth or sixth grade, but take him on to perfection so you will not be ashamed of your work as a teacher. That we may present EVERY MAN perfect in Christ Jesus. I would not say this if Paul had not said it, but since he points it out to us I feel under obligations to lead an army of the same type to make a clean sweep— find every creature, baptize all nations, teach all nations, present every man perfect in Christ Jesus.

This may not be so impossible as it may look to be. When one looks through the pages of the Book instead of the narrowness of his own vision the things of God look different. There is enlargement. It was Joel that was moved by the Holy Ghost according to the way Peter put it that declared God is going to pour out His Spirit upon all flesh. This then, would indicate that He is after all of them in that way at the same time His hunters are searching for the creatures. And it will be noted also that Jesus in telling what the Holy Spirit will do when He comes, or when He is poured out on all flesh, He will reprove the world of sin, and of righteousness and of judgment. Peter declared that this wonderful overflow of the Spirit is to be in the last days, and Jesus says He will reprove the world. Then

I take it that none will escape this mighty work of the
Holy Spirit. Then why not look for and expect these mighty
things instead of all the time putting them off in the future? We surely believe it is God that is stirring us up
to believe we are drawing very near to Paul's dispensation
of the fullness of times when the mighty gathering together
time is come.

Why crawl along on the ice any longer? Why not stand
bolt upright and let this world know who we are, what we
are here for and what we are going to do? Where did
we get the knowledge that gives us such boldness? The
same Holy Spirit that ruled the prophets, and caused them
to speak as they did, has come upon us and illuminated the
Word. He moved the prophets to speak and write, and now
we have caught the spell until we feel we are fully able
to take the world and subjugate it to our Christ and turn
His enemies into His footstool. And God told Jesus to stay
right there at His right hand until His enemies are made
His footstool. Then it is to be noted that the Church is called
into service for the purpose of subduing His enemies while
He remains at His headquarters post—at the right hand of
the Father. Read the marvelous verses: "The LORD said
unto my Lord, Sit thou at my right hand, until I make thine
enemies thy footstool. The LORD shall send the rod of thy
strength out of Zion (the Church): rule thou in the midst
of thine enemies. Thy people shall be willing in the day
of thy power, in the beauties of holiness from the womb
of the morning: thou hast the dew of thy youth." (Psa.
110:1-3)

The statement which tells of the Lord's people being willing in the day of His power agrees with similar statements
which point to a drawing power that will so effect the multitudes that they will come to the Church like flood waters
pour into the larger streams and on into the ocean.
There is the Holy Spirit to be poured out upon all flesh.
There He goes to reprove the world. There goes the last
days message to every creature. Then there is the grace
that brings salvation and will be so powerful and thick that
it can be seen. I tell you, there are wonderful events
scheduled for only a little way up the road. When that grace

floods the world and bathes all men in its lucid waves, and His people sure enough become a willing people, what else can we expect but water poured out upon the thirsty and floods upon the dry ground? It is no wonder that Nebuchadnezzar got such a thrill out of his dream when he saw the stone which represented the Church of the last days as it whisked through the collection of iron, clay, brass, silver and gold (every kind of religion) and crushed the mass together and then the wind carried them away so there was no place found for them. "And the stone that smote the image became a great mountain, and filled the whole earth." (Daniel 2:35) There was a picture worth gazing upon. This vision agrees with all the prophecies on this particular subject. And there are plenty of them.

This image that was crushed by the stone was bright, beautiful and attractive. It was so terrible that it seemed impregnable. Nothing could overthrow it. And the material of which it was composed was non-perishable—gold, silver, brass, iron, clay. There it stood in defiance of any force strong enough to cope with it. Nothing would attempt it. Its very appearance would baffle any attempt. In fact, there was no occasion for a conflict and overthrow. All of the systems of religion of the world today are considered as imperishable as gold and the other materials of which the image was composed. Nebuchadnezzar had a long time of looking at that bright and dazzling beauty. But after many centuries, yea a few thousand years, when the Church got in good headway, according to the powerful spread as described by the prophets and making rapid strides in the twentieth century, at last the feet went to pieces, then down tumbled the brass, the silver, and the gold all in a heap and became as chaff. Then all of that powerful combination of systems became so light and worthless that the pleasant evening breeze carried them away. Even after the systems entirely disappeared the stone kept on swelling and expanding till it filled the whole earth.

I am attempting to show that there is a body of people in the land today who are following so closely in step with prophecy that they are becoming almost wrecklessly brave in their declarations as they sing, "Old Satan, your kingdom must come down," without fear of failure because the Book cannot fail. All the members of this body of people have entered into a sacred covenant that they will take that Book as their only rule of faith and practice. They declare that they stand unequivocally for the whole Bible rightly divided. They cannot go back. They are pledged to go forward to success and victory. The sacred pledge and covenant binds us to put the Church of God in all the world—"the stone (the Church) that smote the image (destroyed all false systems), became a great mountain (government), and filled the whole earth." And Daniel told Nebuchadnezzar that he watched it in his dream till it was all done. Well, it will be done and not so long off either.

But if it is a fact that Jesus will remain at the right hand of His Father till His enemies are made His footstool we surely do not need to look for Him to come tonight. These false systems represented by the image are all more or less against Him. They are His enemies. They must be crushed and blown away. But that is not our discussion here. Our object is getting the souls for our Christ. It is our work to gather the men and women into this stone that is now spreading at such a rapid rate of speed. Bring them in— compel them to come in until the house is full! The last part of this drama is to be carried on by force. The Book that we are pledged to obey says, "compel them to come in." Some will still try to hold on to the former teaching of "whosoever will let him come." That had its place all right, but in the last run it is compel, now isn't it?

Going back to whosoever will let him come, please notice that if you stop there, that arrangement was broken into when Paul was converted. He did not aim to get converted. He was possibly as strong an enemy of Christ as any living today, but he was brought down right there in the road against his will. Others have already been forced down under the power of God in our day against their will. Bring them—compel them till the house is full.

It is very clear that the first shower of the Holy Ghost developed into a flood tide when on the very first day three thousand, one hundred and twenty were drenched, then possibly the next day if not the same afternoon, five thousand more were flooded with the fire from heaven, and then multitudes both of men and women. This wave of the Holy Ghost flood came so suddenly that they scarcely had time to consider whether they wanted it or not. Then it is acknowledged by all that when the former and latter rain is poured out together in the last days that the Church will far exceed in power and glory that of the early Church. The early Church may have reached five or eight thousand a day, and added to the Church daily also. This is what our Book says. Exceeding that good and glorious work in proportion, why not think of reaching a million a day? I asked my secretary to figure for me. I gave her the figures and what do you suppose? To my astonishment she figured that at that rate—that is, a million a day, the Church would knock down the image, crush the life out of all false systems, and fill the earth in five years.

We are not prepared for that rate of speed yet, but we are making mighty strides. And we want to be so well organized and fully prepared that we will be ready for that mighty sweep when it comes. We must work with all our might to get everything set so that when God does pour out His Spirit upon all flesh, and that Spirit does just what Jesus said He would do—"Reprove the world (the whole world) of sin," and the grace of God that bringeth salvation appears to all men—all men, then you can look out for a million souls a day. Then will be fulfilled that all who call upon the name of the Lord shall be saved. And they will call when they are down under a sluice of that reproof and another covering of that grace that can be seen. Paul called when he was felled to the ground like a tree. And Jesus never asked him one time if he was willing. It did not matter whether he was willing or not. Jesus told him to "arise, and go into the city, and it shall be told thee what thou must do." This agrees with bring, and compel —must. I tell you right now, there is going to be something doing when Nebuchadnezzar's image is crushed and all of their papers, books, theories and all other paraphernalia are blown away. All resistance gone. The Church will have all the might there is. Then we can look out for other fulfillments in as many ways as the prophets have described.

Among these will be the lifting up of the ensign to the nations from far, and God will hiss unto them from the end of the earth, and here they will come with speed swiftly.

Now, since these mighty things are only a little way ahead of us, it is our duty to straighten our organization, get everything set so our movements toward the goal can be at a more rapid rate of speed. Every member a worker must be emphasized. Every pastor must learn how to be a pastor instead of only a Sunday preacher. Every evangelist must be so trained that only sickness and death can keep him off of the field. All must be so well trained to pay their tithes and make offerings until money will be supplied to meet the requirements. All members must be trained by the pastor and through the A. B. M. to live such good lives that outside people will be drawn in with their gold and silver—their wealth to help us spread and spread till Nebuchadnezzar can fully see the reality of his dream as he turns over in his grave when he hears the trumpet sound that will awaken the sleeping nations. Then when Daniel walks out and realizes the truthfulness of his interpretation of the dream, I imagine I can see those mighty men that served in their part of the program as they take one another by the hand. And this in the resurrection when the dead in Christ shall rise first and we are changed in a moment and all caught up together in the clouds to meet the Lord in the air.

And beloved, we must make our plans to get the multiplied millions in the Church instead of thinking of only a few. We must get away from traditions and be up-to-date in every way. The old theory of whosoever will and you can't compel, and that straight is the gate and narrow is the way and few there be that find it, must be exchanged for the last days prophecy where we are told that we shall be multiplied and shall not be few.

Stick to the Doctrine

and Win

The Words of Christ Must Be Adhered to by Those Who Are True

NO VACILLATION OR DRAWING BACK

And who wouldn't want to stick to it when it came from the Son of God, the Saviour of the world? He that spake as never man spake astonished the people with His doctrine because He taught them as one having authority and not as uncertain, as was the case with the scribes. He taught them by straight-out words, and also taught by the use of parables to illustrate His teachings and to make His points simple and plain. In His plain talk He said some things that would appear quite strange and pointed. But He did not say them to allow them to be brushed aside as if they were meaningless. Every word He spake was for the special purpose for which it was sent forth. He never spoke words for naught. As He closed that memorable sermon on the mount, the people were so astonished that special mention was made of it and preserved for us to read:

"And it came to pass, when Jesus had ended these sayings, the people were astonished at his doctrine: For he taught them as one having authority, and not as the scribes." (Matt. 7:28, 29)

In closing He gave the story of the difference in building the house upon the rock and on the sand. He made it clear that the house upon the rock would stand the storm while the one built upon the sand would fall when the storm beat upon it. And this story was given to illustrate and put home some truths He had spoken and statements He had made. He declared in His doctrine that those who heard

His message and put His teaching into practice would remain firm and faithful in times of oppositions and storms, while those who failed to put in practice His teachings would fall when the storms of opposition came, like the house built upon the sand.

When I say "stick to the doctrine and win" I mean to not only know His doctrine but put it into practice as well. And this is what every member of the Church of God about which we write and talk has obligated himself to do. Not only to hear but do. And doing the doctrine is sticking to it. And sticking to it, by doing it, we will always win. Whoever, therefore, does just what Jesus says do, will be the winner. And the structure he puts up will not fall down when the storms of oppositions arise. The two important verses to notice in the closing of that wonderful sermon are these:

"Therefore whosoever heareth these sayings of mine, and doeth them I will liken him unto a wise man, which built his house upon a rock." (Matt. 7:24)

"And every one that heareth these sayings of mine, and doeth them not, shall be likened unto a foolish man, which built his house upon the sand." (Matt. 7:26)

These statements by our Lord are positive. It is no wonder the people that heard Him were astonished. He was positive. He meant just that. And He still means just that these many centuries later. There is no change in His authority. He did speak as one having authority, and His message has reached us away down here. Wonderful words they are. Wonderful speaker He was to carry on through the centuries and reach us. And we have obligated ourselves by taking the covenant to do whatsoever He says unto us by His word spoken so many centuries ago. Another positive statement just before He gave the story of the two men—one wise and the other foolish—is in place here and is indeed very important. Read:

"Not every one that saith unto me, Lord, Lord, shall enter into the kingdom of heaven; but he that doeth the will of my Father which is in heaven." (Matt. 7:21)

And Jesus always spoke the will of the Father. And it
is the will of the Father for us to hear and obey Jesus.
This is reiterated by many Scriptures. Thus the Church
of God stands for a close adherence to the words of Jesus
by its members. Then, wise or unwise, which? Hearing
and doing is wise. Hearing and not doing is foolish. Then
when I hear Him say "healing by the power of God for
bodily sickness" and I follow the prescription as laid down
by the Bible I am a wise man. Then when I heard Him say
"healing by the power of God" and I call a physician and
take his medicines I am a foolish man. It is either wise
or foolish. On the rock or on the sand. For my part, I
have chosen to be wise. For forty years I have trusted the
Bible way for healing. I know it is safe. Hear Jesus again
as He says:

"Many will say to me in that day, Lord, Lord, have we
not prophesied in thy name? and in thy name have cast
out devils? and in thy name done many wonderful works?
And then will I profess unto them I never knew you: depart from me, ye that work iniquity." (Matt. 7:22, 23)

And these words follow immediately after the verse that
requires the doing of the will of the Father, or doing the
doctrine of Jesus, to enter into the kingdom. These words
should call people to their senses if they have so far lost
out, or have wandered so far from the Bible as to resort
to medicine in time of sickness, or allowed themselves to
be whisked away to the hospital for attention there. There
are two ways provided by the Bible for healing and these
are given in Mark 16:18 and James 5:13-16. What do people want Bibles for and not do what they say? This would
be like Jesus said at another time that is not to be over-
looked.

"And why call ye me, Lord, Lord, and do not the things
which I say?" (Luke 6:46)

If I were to resort to some other way for healing than
that set forth in the Scriptures, I think I would quit calling on the Lord for anything else. I do not want to be
classed with the foolish man that built his house on the
sand. I have stuck to the rock foundation all these years and

I think it will hold me through all the storms of life that may blow. I have boldly declared myself for the Bible—the words of Jesus—and I shall stick to the doctrine and win. This is not only for healing, but for all it says including the words spoken by Him that spake as never man spake. And I do not hesitate to say that the words of Christ MUST be adhered to by those who are true. And to not do this would be proof of disloyalty and that they are untrue—not true. I tell you, I am in this for all it means! And I mean for all of our people—members—to mean this with no vacillation or drawing back. We have promised to practice the Bible, then we must do it to the man. I am against putting our hands to the plow and looking back. Jesus said, "Remember Lot's wife." And that scares me, for I have no desire or interest in being turned into a pillar of salt and left standing there as a monument of disloyalty and disobedience, yea and rebellion, for the following generations to look upon with disgust. No, never! No, never!! And I do not intend to let any of our people go that way. That's why I am working so hard to train them to be loyal and obedient to our Jesus at all times, just as they promised to do when they joined the Church of God.

Other verses spoken by Him that spake as never man spake are to be considered. Not only is it necessary to practice healing after the Bible order, but all the other instructions and commands He gives as well.

The man or woman then that will not do the things He says they should do, does not love Him, even if they do claim they do. What then is the use for people to claim they love the Lord when they will not do the things He says? This puts some people in a close box when they just will not pay tithes or engage in feet washing or participate in the Lord's supper. I think such people are to be pitied because they surely do not know that when they will not do the things He says they prove they do not love Him. And some of this class may make a loud profession of religion.

There is yet another phase of this subject to which I wish to refer. People are surely either friends of Jesus or straight-out enemies. If I am a friend of Jesus then I will keep His commandments. I am become an enemy if I refuse to do as He gives orders. This view is expressed in the following strong and powerful words though they are only a few.

"Ye are my friends, if ye do whatsoever I command you." (John 15:14)

Now when we think of these things as we should, they are surely quite serious. And the words of Jesus are always pure words, and not to be despised. And I am so anxious to have everyone of our members to be true and loyal at all times and in all things. Stick to the doctrine and win, or reject the doctrine and suffer defeat that will lead to darkness and despair. Let me repeat that the words of Christ must be adhered to by those who are true. And I feel that our people must be true to the promise they made when they became members. I feel under heavy obligations to persuade, to teach, to instruct and help them every way I can. I am afraid some may not have fully understood what they promised. In that case, the pastors, and all of us who do understand, should try to aid them until they get a clear understanding of what they promised when they became members. I am afraid too many have joined the Church of God as they have joined other churches— to leave if they get dissatisfied. This, too, is a serious mistake, because the Church of God is not like other churches. I tell you it will not do to play fast and loose with God or with His Church, either. That is quite dangerous, and on this account I feel we must take all the necessary time that is required to show and teach our people for their own help and benefit. And the weaker ones need the most care and help to lift them up to be equal in strength with the stronger ones.

By His speaking as He did Jesus won the hearts of many. He was gentle and loving, kind and generous, full of compassion and always ready to offer words of sympathy and pity. He healed their sick, fed the multitudes when they were hungry, and ministered to any who had need of His assistance. Loving Saviour. He came to seek and to save that which was lost. He came not to be ministered unto

but to minister. What a Saviour! And we are to be like
Him. By our goodness to others and kind treatment to
them we win. In all of our work and ministry we stick to
the doctrine and never sidetrack, draw back, falter or fail.
There is always a way to deal with every soul to win it
for the Master. By following so close in His footsteps we soon
become so we may attract attention because we show and
express our love in a manner that cannot be resisted.

I only wish I could express myself in the same velvety
manner that I feel while delivering this message. Catch-
ing men and dragging them out of sin is our mission in
this world. It is not enough to give the message and leave
it with them. We must win them. We must save them.
This cannot be done by argument. It is to be done in some
way by love. Tenderness and kindliness go a long way.
Keep up this tender manner of meeting and conversing with
people, and giving them sound doctrine and surely just
around the corner it will be said of us, they speak so different from the other people with whom we mingle.

Remember that we win by love, tenderness, and by sticking to the doctrine and practices marked out by Him we
have been called to follow. Yes, we must win them! We
must win them for our Saviour and then keep them after
they are won. Oh how careful we must be not to offend
—not to be repulsive in our actions and conversation. Our
preaching, too, must be clear and tender, but positive and
without any fears of failure. In quietness and confidence
shall be our strength. I do not know failure. I do not intend for our workers to be of that kind that give up, retreat or suffer defeat. Oh such a sweetness that is taking possession of my spirit as I say, Stick to the doctrine
of our loving Saviour and win. Win souls for Him!

There is a cluster of Scripture verses that properly belong to this subject to which I wish to refer. The first one
calls attention to the importance of the preachers sticking to the doctrine so they can have success and save themselves besides. This infers that any deviation from the
proper course may meet with defeat and disaster.

"Take heed unto thyself, and unto the doctrine; continue

in them: for in doing this thou shalt both save thyself, and them that hear thee." (1 Tim. 4:16)

"If any man teach otherwise, and consent not to wholesome words, even the words of our Lord Jesus Christ, and to the doctrine which is according to godliness; He is proud, knowing nothing, but doting about questions and strifes of words, whereof cometh envy, strife, railings, evil surmisings, Perverse disputings of men of corrupt minds, and destitute the truth, supposing that gain is godliness: from such withdraw thyself." (1 Tim. 6:3-5)

"Jesus answered them, and said, My doctrine is not mine, but his that sent me. If any man will do his will, he SHALL know of the doctrine, whether it be of God, or whether I speak of myself." (John 7:16, 17)

The next verse I shall give shows further importance of sticking to the doctrine in order to be successful in winning and saving even those who would undertake to speak or take a stand against us in our work and service for the Master:

"Holding fast the faithful word as he hath been taught, that he (the minister) may be able by sound doctrine both to exhort and to convince the gainsayers." (Titus 1:9)

As a last Scripture reference for this important subject which terminates in a warning to all of us I wish to bring John on the stand for the purpose of securing special information that every worker needs.

"And this is love, that we walk after his commandments. This is the commandment, That, as ye have heard from the beginning, ye should walk in it. For many deceivers are entered into the world, who confess not that Jesus Christ is come in the flesh. This is a deceiver and an antichrist. Look to yourselves, that we lose not those things which we have wrought, but that we receive a full reward. Whosoever transgresseth, and abideth not in the doctrine of Christ, hath not God. He that abideth in the doctrine of Christ, he hath both the Father and the Son. If there come any unto you, and bring not this doctrine, receive him not into your house, neither bid him God speed: For he that biddeth him God speed is partaker of his evil deeds." (2 John 6-11)

Surely everyone that this message reaches will see the importance of sticking to the doctrine in order to win. And surely it will have a tendency to make us all feel that the sacred words of our Saviour must be adhered to, and that there must be no vacillation or drawing back. We have the message and must stick to it and win. This is the doctrine of the apostles (Acts 2:42) and with which the early Church filled Jerusalem. (Acts 5:28) Hallelujah! Amen!

The Gentiles A Chosen People, Too

And God Is Doing Wonders With And Amongst His Chosen People

WHAT A PRICE THE JEWS PAID FOR THE GENTILES

Oh the glorious wonders described in God's Book! Many of the mysteries contained therein are still hidden, but glimpses of some of them cause thrills to chase through one's entire being sometimes at almost lightning rapidity. What happened to me a moment ago to start this subject would beggar description. It is enough to say that while I was busying myself with some other office work, all of a sudden I found myself pulled away from that delving into this subject as if some supernatural force was directing me.

As I look deeper into it before I have time to any more than start the message, tears begin to fill my eyes. I can scarcely describe my feelings, neither can I find words to express the world of glories and wonders that flashed across my vision as this subject came before me in panoramic style. I am ready to honor the Holy Ghost at all times in revealing God's Book with its mysteries and glories. Indeed there is no other way for it to be known but by the Holy Ghost. Blessed Book! Precious Book! Wonders upon wonders wrapt up in its precious pages, only to be made known by the same Holy Ghost that inspired the writers to write it at the first.

It is generally known that Israel, which finally winds up in the Jews—the other tribes without present day identification—were God's chosen people. The call of Abraham, the dealings with Isaac and Jacob, with all of the history in connection therewith, give proof that this view is correct. That God had a specially chosen people through whom He operated in ancient days is without question. And that He still operates through His chosen people need not be discussed, because this is plain enough to ward off any likelihood of controversy.

Before going further with this subject I wish to give a few verses of Scripture to verify some of the statements made. I wish to call special attention to Abraham, Isaac and Jacob. I wish to show by the Scriptures that these men were specially chosen to fulfill the will of God. A high and sacred calling indeed, but surely not any more so than that of others who have been called and chosen in other generations and decades. The record gives a brief description of the call of Abraham whose name at the first was Abram. Read about it:

"Now the Lord had said unto Abram, Get thee out of thy country, and from thy kindred, and from thy father's house, unto a land that I will shew thee: And I will make of thee a great nation, and I will bless thee, and make thy name great; and thou shalt be a blessing: And I will bless them that bless thee, and curse him that curseth thee: and in thee shall all families of the earth be blessed." (Gen. 12:1-3)

I now wish to call attention to Isaac, Abraham's son, and show how he was a link in the chain and specially chosen as well as his father Abraham.

"And there was a famine in the land, beside the first famine that was in the days of Abraham. And Isaac went unto Abimelech king of the Philistines unto Gerar. And the Lord appeared unto him, and said, Go not down into Egypt; dwell in the land which I shall tell thee of: Sojourn in this land, and I will be with thee, and will bless thee; for unto thee, and unto thy seed, I will give all these countries, and I will perform the oath which I sware unto Abraham thy father; And I will make thy seed to multiply as the stars of heaven, and will give unto thy seed all these countries; and in thy seed shall all the nations of the earth be blessed; Because that Abraham obeyed my voice, and kept my charge, my commandments, my statutes, and my laws." (Gen. 26:1-5)

I shall now proceed to give a few verses that tell about
Jacob as he came on the scene in the drama. God's call and
promises to him were similar to those given to Abraham and
Isaac. The description I shall give is only brief, but sufficient for our present use in connection with this subject and
his part at that time. Read,

"And Jacob went out from Beersheba, and went toward
Haran. And he lighted upon a certain place, and tarried
there all night, because the sun was set; and he took of the
stones of that place, and put them for his pillows, and lay
down in that place to sleep. And he dreamed, and behold
a ladder set up on the earth, and the top of it reached to
heaven: and behold the angels of God ascending and descend-
ing on it. And, behold, the Lord stood above it, and said,
I am the Lord God of Abraham thy father, and the God of
Isaac: the land whereon thou liest, to thee will I give it, and
to thy seed; And thy seed shall be as the dust of the earth,
and thou shalt spread abroad to the west, and to the east,
and to the north, and to the south: and in thee and in thy
seed shall all the families of the earth be blessed. And, behold, I am with thee, and will keep thee in all places whither
thou goest, and will bring thee again into this land; for I
will not leave thee, until I have done that which I have
spoken to thee of." (Gen. 28:10-15)

It was years after this incident and experience that Jacob's
name was changed to Israel which in reality instituted the
house of Israel. Years later Joseph was taken by his brothers
and sold to a caravan of Ishmeelites who carried him into
Egypt and sold him as a slave. The whole story of Joseph
is of thrilling interest. It was through Joseph and the famine
over the entire country that brought the house of Israel
into Egypt and finally put them into bondage and slavery
by a Pharaoh that knew not Joseph. This was in fulfillment
of Genesis 15:13. A reading of a few verses of Scripture
tells the story briefly.

"And Jacob was left alone, and there wrestled a man with
him until the breaking of the day. And when he saw that
he prevailed not against him, he touched the hollow of his
thigh; and the hollow of Jacob's thigh was out of joint, as

he wrestled with him. And he said, Let me go, for the day breaketh. And he said, I will not let thee go, except thou bless me. And he said unto him, What is thy name? And he said, Jacob. And he said, Thy name shall be called no more Jacob, but Israel: for as a prince hast thou power with God and with men, and hast prevailed." (Gen. 32:24-28)

"And Judah said unto his brethren, What profit is it if we slay our brother, and conceal his blood? Come, and let us sell him to the Ishmeelites, and let not our hand be upon him; for he is our brother and our flesh. And his brethren were content. Then there passed by Midianites merchantmen; and they drew and lifted up Joseph out of the pit, and sold Joseph to the Ishmeelites for twenty pieces of silver: and they brought Joseph into Egypt."

It was years after this that Jacob with all his family went down into Egypt where Joseph cared for them during the famine. And now the family name is established as Israel, God's chosen people.

Now our subject makes the statement that the Gentiles are a chosen people, too. The truthfulness of this statement is verified by several Scriptures, both in the Old and New Testaments. And it is surely just as true that the Gentiles have their place as God's chosen people as well as Israel. I will give only a few verses. Read,

"Thus saith the Lord God, Behold, I will lift up mine hand to the Gentiles, and set up my standard to the people." (Isa. 49:22)

"And after they had held their peace, James answered, saying, Men and brethren, hearken unto me: Simeon hath declared how God at the first did visit the Gentiles, to take out of them a people for his name. And to this agree the words of the prophets; as it is written, After this I will return, and will build again the tabernacle of David, which is fallen down; and I will build again the ruins thereof, and I will set it up: That the residue of men might seek after the Lord, and all the Gentiles, upon whom my name is called, saith the Lord, who doeth all these things." (Acts 15:13-17)

"That the Gentiles should be fellowheirs, and of the same body, and partakers of his promise in Christ by the gospel." (Eph. 3:6)

"Then Paul and Barnabas waxed bold, and said, It was necessary that the word of God should first have been spoken to you: but seeing ye put it from you, and judge yourselves unworthy of everlasting life, lo, we turn to the Gentiles. For so hath the Lord commanded us, saying, I have set thee to be a light of the Gentiles, that thou shouldest be for salvation unto the ends of the earth. And when the Gentiles heard this, they were glad, and glorified the word of the Lord: and as many as were ordained to eternal life believed." (Acts 13:46-48)

All of these verses indicate God's call going forth to the Gentiles just as truly as His call was made to Abraham, Isaac and Jacob and all Israel.

Yes, 'tis true, Israel was God's chosen people and He was tender and kind to them and carried them through the wilderness in His arms and fed them with angel's food, gave them flesh to eat and gave them water at times when they were famishing for drink. They were as precious in His sight as the apple of His eye. Oh how tenderly and lovingly God dealt with His chosen people! The above description is verified by the following verses, Read,

"And in the wilderness, where thou hast seen how that the Lord thy God bare thee, as a man doth bear his son, in all the way that ye went, until ye came into this place." (Deut. 1:31)

"Ye have seen what I did unto the Egyptians, and how I bare you on eagles' wings, and brought you unto myself." (Ex. 19:4)

"For the Lord's portion is his people; Jacob is the lot of his inheritance. He found him in a desert land, and in the waste howling wilderness; he led him about, he instructed him, he kept him as the apple of his eye." (Deut. 32:9, 10)

And now since the Gentiles have become His chosen people He is showing mercy and loving kindness to them.

And God is doing wonders with and amongst His chosen people in these days. And it is true that the Gentiles are coming to the brightness of the rising of the Church of God as saith the Scriptures. Some of the Jews may come, but the flood tide that will come to it will be composed of Gentiles. This statement is verified by many Scriptures among which is Romans the ninth chapter. A careful reading of this entire chapter may help us to see still further into the fact that the Gentiles are chosen by the Lord as His people for the last days. And Paul certainly saw just what I am trying to show when he exclaimed,

"I say the truth in Christ, I lie not, my conscience also bearing me witness in the Holy Ghost, That I have great heaviness and continual sorrow in my heart. For I could wish that myself were accursed from Christ for my brethren, my kinsmen according to the flesh." (Rom. 9:1-3)

This is to say that Paul saw how God was turning His favor away from the Jews and lavishing it upon the Gentiles. And this calls for another Scripture to show Paul's reason for loving his own people, the Jews, well enough to be willing to take the curse upon himself that had been placed upon the Jews. And now my eyes moisten with tears as I think of what a price the Jews paid for the Gentiles. It seems almost too much as I make this wonderful discovery. Now for the verses:

"In all their affliction he was afflicted, and the angel of his presence saved them: in his love and in his pity he redeemed them; and he bare them, and carried them all the days of old. But they rebelled, and vexed his holy Spirit: therefore he was turned to be their enemy, and he fought against them." (Isa. 63:9, 10)

Again I say, what a price the Jews paid for the Gentiles! Amazing wonder! Words fail me here. I am afraid I will be unable to convey to other minds the full truth in connection with this message. In a former message I attempted to convey to others the great price paid for the Church and the high value our Lord had placed upon those composing it. Now I am trying to show what a high price the Jews paid for the Gentiles. To describe this a little more fully

I wish to call attention to some more of Paul's discoveries which caused him to exclaim,

"O the depth of the riches both of the wisdom and knowledge of God! how unsearchable are his judgments, and his ways past finding out!" (Rom. 11:33)

Please follow me now into some of these further discoveries and see how indebted we are to the Jews because of the high price they paid to make way for the Gentiles. The high price in this case comes from the fact that when Jesus came to His own (the Jews) they received Him not. The curse was upon them and therefore they could not accept Him. However, a small remnant did accept Him as also saith the Scripture.

"Though the number of the children of Israel be as the sand of the sea, a remnant shall be saved." (Rom. 9:27)

Now a remnant means a very small part of the whole of anything. Or that which is left after the greater part has been removed. And the greater part of the Jews were so far removed from God that when they demanded that Christ be crucified they cried out vehemently with one voice, "Away with him and let His blood be upon us and upon our children." Oh what a curse they were calling upon themselves and their children by that very exclamation! And again let me say, what a price the Jews paid for the Gentiles! Read again,

"When Pilate saw that he could prevail nothing, but that rather a tumult was made, he took water, and washed his hands before the multitude, saying, I am innocent of the blood of this just person: see ye to it. Then answered all the people, (composed of the Jews) and said, His blood be on us, and on our children." (Matt. 27:24, 25)

It can be no wonder that so many millions of Jews have perished, not only in the terrible siege of Jerusalem about forty years later, but all along from that time until even in our day. They were scattered into all the nations of the earth and have suffered untold agonies as their punishments were heaped upon them. They have been a people without a country from that time until now. And really long be-

fore the time of the crucifixion of Christ. But all of this
suffering is the price that they paid for the Gentiles. It is
to be remembered that the Jews were broken off because of
unbelief so that the Gentiles might be grafted in. Now read
from Paul at this point.

"I say then, Have they (the Jews) stumbled that they
should fall? God forbid: but rather through their fall salvation is come unto the Gentiles." (Rom. 11:11)

"Thou wilt say then, The branches were broken off, that
I might be graffed in. Well; because of unbelief they were
broken off, and thou standest by faith." (Rom. 11:19, 20)

"Behold therefore the goodness and severity of God: on
them (the Jews) which fell, severity; but toward thee, (the
Gentiles) goodness, if thou continue in his goodness: otherwise thou also shalt be cut off." (Rom. 11:22)

"As concerning the gospel, they (the Jews) are enemies for
your (the Gentiles) sakes." (Rom. 11:28)

Surely it is plainly seen that the Gentiles are a chosen
people, too. And God is doing wonders with and amongst
His chosen people. And oh what a price the Jews paid for
the Gentiles! Surely we are of great value to the Lord to be
purchased at such a cost to the Jews. And think for a moment how God has worked things after the counsel of His
own will for centuries and ages for our benefit that we
might receive His favor and assistance in making special
preparations for the return of our Lord. Oh how we should
love Him and serve Him faithfully! How we should live
up to the high calling whereunto He has called us! Read:

"Now all these things happened unto them (Israel, the
Jews) for ensamples: and they are written for our admoni-
tion, upon whom the ends of the world are come." (1 Cor.
10:11)

"Thou shalt arise, and have mercy upon Zion (the Church):
for the time to favour her, yea, the set time, is come." (Psa.
102:13)

"For he will finish the work, and cut it short in righteousness: because a short work will the Lord make upon the earth." (Rom. 9:28)

"The zeal of the Lord of hosts will perform this." (Isa. 9:7)

And since we are His representatives or ambassadors He is depending upon us to do the work. And since we as the Gentiles are chosen for this special work in the last days we must hasten on and finish the work with which we are entrusted. And the great work is to put the Gospel of the kingdom (power) in all the world and finish it up in due time. And we should keep in mind the high price paid for us, both the blood of Jesus and the terrible suffering that came upon the Jews that we could be grafted in and God's favor heaped upon us.

Who is Who?

All Should Submit To Authority After The Bible Order

SOME HAVE FORSAKEN THE RIGHT WAY TO THEIR OWN HURT

Do any of you remember of a conflict coming up between two prominent men of the early Church? The trouble arose between Paul and Barnabas. On their first missionary journey they had John Mark with them for a while, but by and by he became homesick, or concluded the hardships were too great, or the persecutions too severe, or something, and deserted them and went back home. When it was decided to go on a second journey Barnabas insisted on taking the young man with them again, but Paul thought it not good because he forsook them and went back home before. The contention became quite sharp between them. Paul was filling the place as overseer over the churches of that region and Barnabas was a companion in labor. But when this conflict arose between them Barnabas refused to submit to his superior officer. As a result of this parting asunder one from the other, Barnabas took Mark and sailed into Cyprus while Paul chose Silas and departed to his field of labor, where they went about confirming the churches and pushing out into new fields. It was on this trip that Timothy was found and harnessed up in the work.

But the important matter to which I wish to call attention is that concerning Barnabas. His name was there dropped from the record by the historian as if he had died. Luke, the writer of the book of Acts, makes no more mention of him. Had he submitted to Paul, who was over him in the Lord, doubtless his name would have been carried right on in the record. But on account of failing to recog-

nize consituted authority under God's order which He put in
the Church of God, his name was carried no further.

Those who have studied our records have been able to
track quite a number of names up to certain times and
places and then they are not found any further. What is
the cause of this disappearing of names? Well, here it is
in short. When names of ministers have disappeared along
in the records when there is no notation given of their death,
it is a sign that they have failed to submit to God's order
in some manner, and others have enlisted to fill up the
ranks. Some have rebelled against the overseers—those who
are over them in the Lord; some have fallen into heresy
or other errors; some have done just what Paul said they
would do, spoken perverse words to draw away disciples
after them. This class has undertaken to set up something
over which they could have the rule and pre-eminence.

All of these uprisings, rebellions, heresies and names disappearing from the records, have occurred to prove who
is who. John explains it very clearly when he says, "They
went out from us, but they were not of us; for if they
had been of us, they would no doubt have continued with
us: but they went out, that they might be made manifest
that they were not all of us." (1 John 2:19)

In other words, John shows that they went out in order
to show who is who. And this cleansing process is still going on. During the past year some names have been ex-
punged from our records that may never appear again. This
disintegration has been caused by a spirit of rebellion against
constituted or established authority. The minister that blunt-
ly refuses to recognize the authority, instructions, advices
and counsels of the overseer that is over him in the Lord
will sooner or later go on the rocks. It is sorrowful, it is
pitiful to look on the faces of some of these I know, but
they have done it themselves by refusing to submit to the
wise counsel of those who are over them in the Lord. And
the sooner the balance of our people learn who is who according to the Bible way of putting it, the better off they
will be. It is the self-willed, the rebellious, the insincere, those
who despise dominion and government that sooner or later

fall on the rocks and are usually ruined forever. Very few
of such people ever recover. I have seen them try, yes, apparently they have made tremendous efforts only to fall
back again into the whirlpool of discouragement, or still
further and deeper rebellion, to never rise again. Truly it
is a fearful thing to fall into the hands of a living and
angry God. He is determined to have His order of government recognized and obeyed. If some will not do it because they love to have the pre-eminence themselves, He
will let them go to the rocks and get others that will follow His order of government. The minister that stands up
boldly before his congregation and irreverently declares he
is going to do thus and so whether it suits the overseer
or not, and at the same time knowing he is running over
the counsel and advice of him that is over him in the Lord
will sooner or later go on the rocks so his name will disappear from the records in the future.

It might be considered a light thing for Barnabas to have
rejected the counsel and advice of Paul who had evidently
been placed in the position as overseer of the territory to
which they were going, but by his doing so, even that little, left his name off of the record thereafter. And whether
it would be considered a light offence or a grave offence,
the effect was just the same. No more mention of him is
made in the book of Acts. And if he ever did retract, repent and come straight so he served further in the early
Church, there is no mention made of it in Luke's writings,
who was evidently the historian of Church work in those
days. But whether he did or not, this incident is surely a
danger signal hung out to show to others the danger of dis-
regarding the wise counsel of those who are over them in
the Lord.

Paul had good reasons for thinking it was not best for
John Mark to go back over there. He might have acted
in a way that he lost his standing or reputation as a preacher over in that country. Paul felt the responsibility and
wanted things to be carried on in good order in his territory, as every other good state overseer desires. I have
heard some of our state overseers make statements in a
similar manner. Referring to a certain minister they have

said, "I'd rather he would not come into my state." Doubtless Paul knew it was not best for John Mark to go back
over there again. It was the duty of Barnabas to submit to
Paul and let John Mark go to other fields, because it was
Paul's territory as overseer. And even as General Overseer I would not knowingly send a minister into a state contrary to the wishes of a good, dependable and faithful overseer. And when those ministers went up from Jerusalem
to Antioch representing themselves as having been sent by
James to teach that the Gentiles must be circumcised and
keep the law, it was learned afterward that their representa-
tion was false for James declared he never gave them any
such instructions.

It is evident that those false teachers learned who was
who before they got through with James and that council
of apostles and elders, of which James was presiding officer
as well as General Overseer of all the churches, including
the churches in Paul's territory as well as under John,
Peter and all others. I tell you, I am afraid to depart from
God's order. And on the other hand I feel a tremendous
life in my spirit when I speak or write in its defence. I
agree with Paul that it was not best for John Mark to go
on that trip into Paul's territory, without knowing his reasons, because of the position Paul held.

It has been said that some who were our preachers, but
are gone now, used to lay special emphasis on Hebrews 13:17
as long as they could put it to the members of the congregation under them, but when the same rule was to be
applied to them by the overseers who were over them they
disobeyed, rebelled and bolted. Then a few of the state overseers in the past have been very attentive toward having
the ministers in their territory to obey them, but when it
became necessary for the General Overseer to call them to
account and give them counsel, advice and instructions, it
was another thing. And some have even uttered words of
defiance which has thrown them into the rank with those
mentioned by Peter and Jude in their last days' messages
who were not afraid to speak evil of dignities—those who
are above them in rank or position.

"But these, as natural brute beasts, made to be taken and destroyed, speak evil of the things that they understand not; and shall utterly perish in their own corruption." (2 Peter 2:12)

Peter states further that such people have forsaken the right way, which shows they were once in the right way, and were probably good workers in the Master's service. But they have gone wrong some way and gone so far that they utter words of defiance of any rule or authority over them. Then, look out, matters are becoming serious for them, and Peter mentions them as cursed children, wanting more money than they are getting, and will put in practice any kind of a covetous or dark scheme to get it.

All of these references have been given to illustrate who is who after the Bible order. And in concluding this topic I wish to make an attempt to express my gratitude to the many of my fellow helpers and co-workers for their loyalty, stick-to-itiveness, uprightness and co-operation, and for their honor and respect toward their General Overseer. To say I love you is putting it very mild. Many of you have ravished my heart, enchanted and charmed me by your valiant service. Your noble deeds and brilliant victories you have achieved in the hard fought battles, in my estimation have made many of you worthy of a badge of honor and the applause of angels. I say, hurrah for the faithful soldiers who have fought heroically for liberty and truth up to this hour.

The Last Days Are Upon Us

Scripture Prophecies Must Be Fulfilled

WE MAY NOT KNOW THEM ALL BUT WE ARE LEARNING AS THE DAYS GO FLEETING BY

The last days are upon us, there is no room for argument over this question—the Scripture settles it. The anti-Christ spirit is galloping over the world at a rapid rate binding with fetters every person that will give him the least opportunity by deviating from the truth as contained in the Scripture. This statement is confirmed by the Scripture itself. Paul in writing of the dangers of the last days and with a desire to throw out a red light of warning to people who are inclined to be careless about their best interests tells of the anti-Christ spirit and upon whom he will work and shows he fastens his fangs into people who do not love the truth. This cunning one is after the working of Satan and comes "with all deceivableness of unrighteousness in them that perish; because they received not the love of the truth, that they might be saved."

"And for this cause God shall send them strong delusion, that they should believe a lie: That they all might be damned who believed not the truth, but had pleasure in unrighteousness." (2 Thess. 2:10-12)

In the light of this Scripture then we can readily conclude that the anti-Christ spirit is rushing through the land marking the multitudes who do not love the truth contained in the Bible and thus do not conform to its teachings. And where are the people that really prove their love of the truth by their sincere obedience to it?

Further down in this same chapter Paul shows what he means by truth, so we are not left in the dark as to what the truth is that people should love for it is certain that if they do not love it the "strong delusion" is liable to overtake them any day. There is but little room for the sky of this Scripture to be so overcast with clouds that people cannot see if they will only read for themselves and give the matter just consideration. In telling how this anti-Christ spirit may be evaded and how to escape the coils of "strong delusion" he writes:

"Therefore, brethren, stand fast, and hold the traditions which ye have taught, whether by word, or our epistle." (2 Thess. 2:15)

Then we understand that the way to escape the coils of the "strong delusion" and the cruel fangs of the anti-Christ spirit is to love Paul's teaching enough to obey and practice it. And this, of course, will pull us together up to the early Church standard in every particular thing as taught and practiced by Jesus and His holy apostles. Looking at it from this viewpoint, what do you see? Where are the people that are striving for the standard marked out by Paul? Are we all in danger, or are we, as a body, so nearly standing fast and holding to Paul's teachings that we are safe? I read further what Paul says.

"Examine yourselves, whether ye be in the faith; prove your own selves." (2 Cor. 13:5)

And I verily believe it would be wisdom for all of us to take sufficient time to do this so we can be doubly sure that we are continuing "steadfastly in the apostles' doctrine and fellowship." (Acts 2:42) At any rate this is the standard for which we are striving, and we love the truth of this standard well enough to forsake everything else, refuse to compromise, and break for the mountain peaks and make our way thitherward at any cost and sacrifice. But what of others who are making no pretense or claim of even trying to reach such a high altitude? Well, I am not the judge, but two special Scriptures come rushing to my mind. I will give them in the order they came and if they do not apply here, pass them over, but if they do then stand with me quivering under the awe that suddenly appears as I reflect over last days conditions. Here they are for what they are worth:

"For the time is come that judgment must begin at the
house of God: and if it first begin at us, what shall the end
be of them that obey not the gospel of God? And if the
righteous scarcely be saved, where shall the ungodly and
the sinner appear?" (1 Peter 4:17, 18)

"For Moses truly said unto the fathers, A prophet shall
the Lord your God raise up unto you of your brethren,
like unto me; him shall ye hear in all things whatsoever
he shall say unto you. And it shall come to pass, that every
soul, which will not hear that prophet, shall be destroyed
from among the people." (Acts 3:22, 23)

In the light of prophecy and these Scriptures it is certainly time for people who are serving God in a half-hearted
manner to get down to business and quit making a mock
of it. God wants wholehearted service and this is what I
am trying to press our people into whether others do it
or not. Our duty is our duty; our service is our service;
our work is our work, and not the work or service or duty
of somebody else. We must be faithful to Him that called
us and we must not slow down because others are in the
rear. We are bravely marching up the mountain slopes,
earnestly contending for the faith once delivered unto the
saints. And we refuse to lower the standard or let it
trail in the dust. Somebody must keep this faith and I do
not know of any others any more capable or heroic in the
last-days battles than we. And if God is depending upon
us as His messengers to fulfill prophecy then we must not
fail Him, for Scripture prophecies must be fulfilled. We may
not know them all but we are learning as the days go
fleeting by.

"This scripture must needs have been fulfilled," said Peter
in the upper room after they had returned from Bethany
where they had witnessed the Lord depart upward from
them. The Scripture he referred to was the one concerning Judas who had betrayed our Lord into the hands of
the howling mob. Of Judas, Peter said:

"For he was numbered with us, and had obtained part
of this ministry." (Acts 1:17) Then he proceeded to quote
the Scripture closing the quotation as follows:

"Let his habitation be desolate, and let no man dwell there-in: and his bishoprick let another take."

Peter and those with him were acting their part in the drama by calling attention to the prophecy and selecting one to take the place of the traitor. Some have offered to criticise this action of the apostles in selecting Matthias. They say Paul was the proper one. But no, they were only do-ing their part in answer to prophecy. Paul followed on as "one born out of due time" and became an apostle to the Gentiles, but the selection of Matthias was the proper or-der. It was necessary to select one who had companied with them from the baptism of John unto the day Jesus was taken up (Acts 1:21, 22), and Paul had not done that. But the criticism of these people only shows the frailty of man and their disposition to speak things they do not under-stand. It was just as necessary for that Scripture to be fulfilled and one chosen to succeed Judas as the one which told of the coming of John the Baptist (Isa. 40:3; John 1:23) and of the Bethlehem birth of Jesus. (Micah 5:2) Truly Scripture prophecies must be fulfilled and we must fill our place in them just as faithfully as others have done. And surely we have a place in them to fill in the closing up of this age.

Many of us are so sure that the Church is to be re-estab-lished in the last days with only the law and government given by Jesus at the first that we have no hesitancy in declaring it. We find prophecies and teachings to this ef-fect both in the Old and New Testament Scriptures. Our ministers and many of our members are enthusiastic in this opinion, and well they may be because the Scripture prophe-cies must be fulfilled and they can read and the Lord gives understanding.

Taking what might appear to be the last Scripture first we are left with an indisputable right to this claim. Paul is the great Church teacher of the New Testament and reaches the climax as he pictures the Church in a state of perfection to be presented to Christ by the Lord Himself. In this connection he shows that the Church reaches the high state of being subject to Christ in everything and tells also of the purchase of it by giving Himself for it and then adds:

"That he might present it to himself a glorious church, not having spot, or wrinkle, or any such thing; but that it should be holy and without blemish." (Eph. 5:27)

And it may be well said that Paul's falling away (2 Thess. 2:3) has already come, and is in the past, and we are on this side of that condition now. The early Church lost her identity after being subject to Christ in everything in the year 325 when the first creed was accepted and they began to make laws to govern it instead of following the laws already made by Christ Himself and practiced by the holy apostles. And since that time the Lord's people have been scattered and divided and separated by walls and partitions of laws and governments and institutions and constitutions instead of being subject to Christ in everything. The conditions as witnessed in a general sense in these last days are deplorable, but God is moving and has His people at work doing faithful service in the last days revolutionary movement which is destined to so grow in influence and power as to force a decision either in favor of the full and unequivocal obedience to Christ in everything or against this high standard, one or the other. The time is rapidly coming when mere approaches and movements will not satisfy the honest and sincere sheep of God's pasture field. They are going to demand the fulfillment of prophecy to the extent that Isaiah will have to be heard as he proclaims as a mouthpiece for God:

"Judgment also will I lay to the line, and righteousness to the plummet: and the hail shall sweep away the refuge of lies, and waters shall overflow the hiding place." (Isa. 28:17)

This would infer that people must either begin to obey Christ or make no pretense of being a Christian. This stage has not been reached yet, but it is coming sooner or later. God has spoken and He will not go back. The die is cast and what is molded in it will have to fit it. God's Word is unchangeable, so we had just as well begin to measure ourselves by it and adjust ourselves to the inevitable. It

is either do this or get out of the way so the way may
be clear for others who will measure to the Word and obey
it. I wonder if it could be possible that some who have
gone out from us are only getting out of the way so we
can make more rapid strides toward the mark pictured by
both the prophets and apostles. At any rate we feel much
lighter and more fleet of foot as if some weights have been
thrown off. And I wonder if John has not painted a last
days picture when he said:

"Little children, it is the last time: and as ye have heard
that anti-christ shall come, even now are there many anti-
christs; whereby we know that it is the last time." (1 John
2:18)

And then, as if some special event were reserved for or
would take place in the last days, John adds:

"They went out from us, but they were not of us; for if
they had been of us, they would no doubt have continued
with us: but they went out, that they might be made manifest that they were not all of us."

Now this was written for some purpose pertaining to the
last days, and if nothing else it must be for the consolation
of some of the Lord's people whose family relations or close
friends refuse to meet the conditions laid down in Christ's
law and turn away from the truth. Some experiences of this
kind have been very painful already and more of a similar
nature may take place as we near the time of the end of the
age. And this also shows how some may be among us taking part in our services and yet are not really of us. This
view is voiced both by Peter and Jude. (2 Peter 2:13-15; Jude
12) Such things are very grievous and to be deplored, but
they are possible according to these Scriptures. How people can practice deceit like that is something I can't understand, and why people would want to trifle with their souls
and be dishonest when they surely know they can't deceive
the all-seeing eye of God is more than I can explain.

It is evident that we fall under the same critical gaze that
met Paul at Rome when he was told by the Jews who came
to him at his call that he might explain to them the reason
he was there in bonds. During the counsel they said to Paul,

"We neither received letters out of Judaea concerning thee, neither any of the brethren that came shewed or spake any harm of thee. But we desire to hear of thee what thou thinkest: for as concerning this sect, we know that everywhere it is spoken against." (Acts 28:21, 22)

I feel greatly honored to be counted worthy to belong to the very same "sect" that is everywhere spoken against. It adds inspiration to me and adds a glory in my soul because I know we are faithfully following the Scripture teachings relative to the Gospel and the Church of which Paul was a member and which is destined to come to the front in the last days.

Our people have a perfect right, like Paul, to thank God and take courage. (Acts 28:15) Although there will be times that would naturally look gloomy along this ascent to the top of the mountains, yet faith in the prophecies dispels the gloom and we, like the eagles, keep our eyes on the sun and rise above the storm clouds.

Family Worship Every Day

Father, Mother, Children Should Be Closely
United Together in the Master's Service

I think the proper way for a newly married couple to commence housekeeping is with erecting a family altar for family worship and saying grace at the table. Thank the Lord for the food and ask His blessings upon it before a mouthful is eaten. It is true we cannot expect everybody to do this because many are not even saved until later in life, but how much better things would be if this were so! And our people are to train their children while small so when they marry they will expect nothing else but family worship and grace.

I was not raised to pray and love the Bible, but the very first year my wife and I began to keep house and live to ourselves an incident occurred that put our family worship going and it has never ceased to this day. Thanks to God for getting us started off right in that respect. And even now, after forty-eight years have sped by the incident is fresh in my memory. We commenced housekeeping in a little frame house sixteen by twenty on the side of a country road in Hamilton County, Indiana. My mind runs back to that time and place as if it were yesterday. The special feature is the starting of our family worship. True it was a small family, only two of us, but it was enough to claim the promise of Jesus being in the midst.

We were married in April and this incident occurred in July. The hired men and myself were making hay. A storm came up and we ran our wagons into the big hay barn only partly loaded. I left the horses with the men and hastened to the little house about a couple of hundred yards away to be company for my wife during the storm. I reached the

house and ran through the kitchen into the other room and
sat down with my face toward the door that led into the
kitchen which I just came through. Mary was standing in
front of me and we were smiling at each other because I had
reached the house by the time the rain began to fall. Suddenly came a crash—a thunder peal that almost deafened
us. Mary was the first to speak. "That must have struck the
barn," she said. "No, dear, it's closer than the barn, it's our
house."

That ball of fire dropped out of that storm cloud right
into the top of the chimney, down through the cook stove and
out at the lower door and started toward us, but for some
cause it turned right back around the stove and crashed out
through the ceiling and weather-boarding of the house. I
saw it as it came out of the stove and made a dart in our
direction and suddenly stopped as if speaking to us, then
darted back and disappeared. It was a flash of lightning and
did not take as long as it might appear from the way I am
telling it. I felt it was the voice of God. I pondered the
words in my heart like Mary the mother of Jesus. I climbed
up in the attic to see if any fire had started. When the storm
was over I finished my day's work and hurried back to the
house. In a little while I asked my wife for her Bible. I did
not have one. I turned to some place—just any place and
began to read. I said, "It was the voice of God that spoke
to me this afternoon saying, 'read the Bible, pray, start your
family worship tonight!'" The fear of God was upon me. It
was the same with wife. She could have read and prayed,
but I was afraid not to do it myself. My prayer was quite
awkward, but it was enough to start our family worship.

I cannot say that I was saved that night, but we kept on
with our family prayers until God did save me. Only two
of us, which was a small family, but that was the beginning of our family worship. We erected our family altar
and built the fire upon it that has never gone out. For
forty-eight years the family altar fires have never gone out.
I have been away from the home most of my life but that
faithful wife kept the fires burning. When I was on the
mission field and wife was taken sick and I could not get
home to her for so long, the children were trained to keep

the fire burning. They were also faithful in saying grace at the table. Always when I came home I found the altar fires still burning. I have been away from home months at a time, and when I came home I never failed to find wife and all the children keeping up the family prayer. The children grew up in it and have never departed from the practice.

That is one service the Lord put me into before I was ready. I was not knocked down in the road as Paul was, but that flash of lightning was as if God spoke to me. I knew nothing about the Bible. It was a long time after that lightning flash that spoke to me before I read about Paul's experience. I could almost think it was the Lord that spoke to me just as truly as it was He who spoke to Paul. I could hardly give it in terms as Paul did, but it had the effect in starting me out for the Lord and family worship just as really as the flash of light at midday sent Paul to the Gentiles.

We first started our family worship at night just before retiring. This was carried on for years. After we launched out in the Master's service more we changed our worship to the morning. Many times we would have it both night and morning. Then we always prayed at night, each one to ourselves and had the family worship in the morning. When we were out so much at night in revivals and other services we could not get together so well. The morning is still our time for family worship. When I am away wife carries on. Now that the children are grown and have homes of their own, wife still keeps the altar fires burning. When she is alone she reads and prays just as if others were present. When we two are alone we read and pray—just two of us, as when we first started on that memorable night just a few hours after God spoke to us as He did.

Family worship every day. What is more beautiful than for father, mother, children to gather around the altar fire and read while all are quiet, then all kneel together and pray? We used to pray around. I guess my children cannot remember when they began to pray. Then they never did quit. They still keep up their prayers. And don't you think this is a glorious consolation to their parents? So many parents do not have the joy of hearing their children pray. I scarcely know how to sympathize with them because my children have always prayed.

Just here I think of the broken homes. They never learned the pleasure of father, mother and all the children joining in as fast as they grew up and learned to talk. Probably they did not want it that way. Probably they do not want it that way now. It may be possible that I am the only one in the wide world that was called to family prayer by God's voice through a stroke of lightning. Paul is the only one that we ever had any record of that was called to the Gentiles by a flash of light at midday. My experience was just as real. Probably others would have started family worship if God had called them as He did me. I wonder why the Lord was so mindful of me and got me started so early in life when so many others scarcely ever get started—and when such a few families are made happy by having father, mother and children participate in this sacred service all their lives. When I think of this I meditate upon it with a feeling of deep sacredness. I wish I could be the means of starting a thousand families into the sacred service. They need not wait to be started into it by a flash of lightning. I suppose only one will have such a frightful experience to drive him to his knees. Only one couple will be spoken to just in that way, but a thousand couples could surely commence this noble service tonight and never stop it, just as well as we.

Family worship was one of the subjects discussed in our first Assembly held January 26 and 27, 1906. And how singular that I am preparing a message on this subject just thirty-one years later. It will be read by thousands thirty-one years after that discussion. Doubtless it will be exceedingly interesting to read the exact words written concerning that discussion and the result:

"Family worship was discussed by Andrew Freeman and others. It is, therefore, the sense of this assembly that we recommend and urge that the families of all churches engage in this very sacred service as least once a day and at a time most convenient to the household, and that the parents see that every child is taught, as early as possible, to reverence God and their parents by listening quietly and attentively to the reading of God's Word and getting down on their knees during the prayer. We recommend further that the ministers and deacons of each church use their influence and make special effort to encourage every family in the church to engage in this devotional exercise every day. And that the deacons ascertain the proper information and make a report of the number of families that have been induced to take up this service during the year, the number that make it a regular practice and those that do not, and carry such report to the yearly or General Assembly."

Away back there, thirty-one years ago, these were some of the duties assigned the deacons. They were to visit all the families of the local church and encourage them to have their family worship. Then they were required to report their findings at the Annual Assembly each year. This has long since been lost sight of and no such reports are now given at the Assemblies. But I do think every effort should be made to encourage all of our families to have their daily family worship. This is one way to help take care of the children and train them to reverence the Holy Bible and prayer. In the home is the place to train the children to get down on their little knees and close their little eyes and listen reverently while mother and father pray. Then they should be taught to pray some little prayer. For convenience at the close of their family worship the whole family may repeat the prayer in concert that Jesus taught His disciples to pray.

Too often children grow up and get out from under the family government too early—then it is not long till you hear mothers calling for prayers for their children. This could have been avoided if the proper government could have been observed in the home. Father, mother, children, should be closely united in the Master's service, and the place to commence this close union is the family circle and their daily observance of the family worship. I can scarcely think of a more beautiful sight than to see parents and all the children in a group together engaged in family worship. Then the parents have the children under their control. Keep them in family worship as long as they remain at home, and when they get a home of their own they will be very sure to start their own homes with family worship. They could hardly be satisfied without it.

I wish I could be the means of starting a thousand family altars burning by this message. Nobody can say that it's not good. Who would say anything against the father of a family calling his children around him in the capacity of family worship? See that proud father of a well-governed home as he takes up the Bible at the regular hour for worship and the children gathering around without a word being said because they have been trained? Mother has a special place to sit and every child knows its place. Even the baby will stop its cooing long enough for father to read the Scripture lesson. Then watch them all as they get on their knees without being told. This is one picture that used to affect strangers or friends that came into our home to spend the night.

A description of a well-regulated home where the family altar fires burn is given by the Psalmist in Psalm 127:3-5; Psalm 128. Read and think and reflect and pray for others who may not have started this more than wonderful family worship.

I am enthused about family worship the same as I am about all of our other teachings and practices. I think one of the duties of the pastors and deacons is to teach our families to engage in family worship. I think family worship can be made one means of making preparation for the coming of the Lord. I would here say with one of the songs that is sometimes sung, "Do not neglect your family prayer." As I become more and more enthused about family worship and the worth of it for our people, I feel that same kind of feeling that often comes over me when I am touching a subject that I believe God approves. I wonder if it could be a fact that some of our precious fathers and mothers are neglecting their family prayer and thus depriving themselves and their children of one of the most important means of grace provided and recommended by the first Assembly when the light of the last days Church was just beginning to rise over the eastern hills. Come on, friends, let more of us avail ourselves of this means of grace we call FAMILY WORSHIP.

Our Constructive Program

Must Be Continued

Put All of Our Hidden Energy Into Action

THE RESULTS WILL BE MARVELOUS

It has been previously announced that our work was constructive rather than destructive. It is our purpose to build men—lift them up to a higher plane of living and happiness. They sometimes have to be rebuilt. There is rebuilt machinery that does good service for a long time. One of the main objects in building and rebuliding men is to get their service. The Master needs the very best service of all the men and women we can get. His object is to save men. We must get them for Him. It takes real energy of the kinetic type to engage in the constructive work marked out for us by our program. But our constructive program must be continued without the least bit of abatement. It just will not do to let the work drag or even slow down to the very least degree.

How many would have a tendency to be like a bullet shot upward out of a gun? It is making the greatest speed as it leaves the muzzle of the gun. The further it mounts upward the slower it rises. It finally reaches a height that it stops completely. Then it is designated as a spent bullet. Its force is all gone. I am afraid too many who have been mighty workers are spent. They have gone to their limit and then began to get slower and slower. We want that kind of energy that gathers speed as it goes and it is never spent. We must not be like the bow that is bent and is never let go to send the arrow to its mark. Doubtless many of our own people have energy that has never been set in motion. Our women of the church are an example. Previous to 1928 when the W. M. B. was instituted our women had just as much energy, perhaps, as they have now, but it was of the potential type. It was like a spring that was clamped down so its force could not do anything. When the clamp was blasted from the women in 1928 by the institution of the Womens Missionary Band they became, as a whole, a mighty factor in raising missionary money, besides the many other ways they have served for the Master.

It is my purpose to stir into action every bit of energy that lies dormant in every member. Look at the water as it has made its way down the winding rivers for centuries. Its energy was wasted and even caused much destruction during floods. But now, since the dams and machinery have been constructed and the water pours down through the channels made for it, see how that once-lazy water is revolutionizing the whole world. The multiplied millions of spindles are whirling at lightning speed in manufacturing the commodities of life. The energy that once operated the old spinning wheel can now be turned into service for God in sending forth the every-creature message to the every creature instead of being spent at the wheel and loom.

I am sure there is enough energy lying dormant in God's people to revolutionize the whole world in a day if it were only put into operation in systematic order so the very best could be expected to effect the greatest amount of good. Leaving out of the picture all but our own Church of God members I do not hesitate to make the statement that with all of our hidden energy put into action the results will be marvelous. This is like another locomotive hooked on to the loaded train; or another team of horses hitched to a loaded wagon, to our policy of every member a worker. This train must hasten on up the grade. This wagon must go on up to the top of the hill. It must! It must! I mean the every-member-a-worker policy must not only win but rush on at ever-increasing speed. Let me repeat that, WITH ALL OF OUR HIDDEN ENERGY PUT INTO ACTION THE RESULTS WILL BE MARVELOUS as we pursue our constructive program.

I have often made the statement in the conventions, that I never expected to stop until every member is a worker. I am still full of that determination. Men of the world are harnessing the waters so every drop of water is a worker to furnish its energy and power to move the mighty machinery. Instead of the water flowing down the stream almost like it was useless it can now boast of its usefulness in that respect as well as many others. Instead of our women just going to the house of worship for a few hours each week with no special work marked out for them to do, as they used to do, they are now a thousand times happier with the big responsibility of raising money with which to gain souls. And they are not as a bullet that is spent, but they are gathering speed as they rush on toward the goal, which is the salvation of the lost souls.

There are no dams and power plants on the little branches and creeks, except it might be for the running of a little water power grist mill. But when the water from these smaller rivulets, branches, creeks and streams flows together and forms a big river, there are the mighty dams and power plants. Just so is the mighty Church of God. There are the small local churches that furnish some of the membership and means. When this means flows together to headquarters it creates a power that is starting its march to move the world. A further comparison is that when all the Christian faiths and movements flow down their little narrow channels until they empty into the Church of God—the Bible Church —what mighty wheels and what mighty machinery will be put into motion to save the world! Every member a worker and a special work for every one. This is the slogan! All of this is just a little way up the road toward the realization and fulfillment of the prayer of our Lord and confirmed by Paul's call to prayer for all men. And if such can never be, why did Jesus pray such a prayer? And if such can never be, why did Paul tell us to pray for all men? I do not believe in men of authority that would mock us like that— tell us to pray for all men and at the same time tell us they won't be saved. Then in Jesus' prayer He shows that the only way to get the world stirred is for all of His own people to become one, and He also shows by His prayer that that is the way to get the balance of the world saved. I say, I don't believe in men of authority that would put us into a job that could not be performed. But, thank heaven, Jesus and Paul mean just what they say, and I am working at our constructive program with perfect assurance that we will win. And all of the energy of every member as every member becomes a worker will perform the task and win the victory.

Please don't think I'm exaggerating just because I have leaped over the bounds of traditions and quote from two men that have far greater authority than traditions ever had or ever will have. I tell you, when all the energy that is now lying dormant in even our own members is stirred up and put into operation under systematic guidance, like the drops of water are guided through the channels that lead to the water wheel, mighty work will be done in a very short period of time. With all of our activities in operation and all of our energies at work, nothing but success can crown our efforts. As we make the long hard dash after the souls of men we cannot think of coming back without them.

Enthused? I guess I am! Why shouldn't I be enthused? And why shouldn't all of our ministers and members be enthused? I can hardly think of any one being a member of this great wonderful institution which is unctionized by God Himself and not be enthused. If they are not, then I would naturally think their energies are of the potential type. That is, they are like the bow that is bent but locked down so the arrow cannot speed away. They are like the waters of the little rill that soak into the ground before they get to the mighty power dams that are away below in one of the big rivers into which they would flow if they should keep on flowing down the stream. Who would want his energies to lie silent as the grave, unused and inactive for a life time, and die with them still asleep and motionless? Not I, O, not I! I hope every member of the Church of God will join me in this and let loose the string that is holding the bow bent and let the arrow fly to its mark— the salvation of souls and the full preparation for the coming of the Lord. It will take all of our energy in action to accomplish the will of God and carry out His eternal program.

Men who are in business keep their nerves strained to the limit almost all the time. They do it to succeed in business and make money. Since men can use such a vast amount of energy to succeed in business, how much more should we put into action all of our energy to save souls! Souls are of vast value and will continue on in eternity, while wealth is to use and satisfy a longing for it for only a short period of time. In order to accomplish the greatest good all of our programmed activities must be kept in operation. It will take energy in operation to accomplish this, I believe it is going to take more of a display of God's power, and a greater display of energy to finish up our part of God's program than has been displayed for any purpose since the world was.

I feel sometimes like I would like to have a connecting rod that would reach every minister so I might check upon their work and service every day. I would call their attention to their activities about every three hours. If they had not done anything for the Master for the first three hours I would urge them to make up for the lost time the next three hours. I would keep their nerves tightened the whole day through. I would want each one to get a soul a day, then later I would call for a soul every half day and keep gaining in skill, wisdom, energy and the power of God until they could report at least a soul an hour. Now this is the way I feel about it. And if I can become so enthusiastically interested, how much more is God interested when it is said of Him that He is not willing for any to perish, but that all should come to repentance. Since He is not willing for any to be lost, and we are His dependence to get them saved through Christ, I think He may be prompting every minister by way of His connecting rod. I am afraid some have been prompted to stir themselves to a greater speed but they have not heeded the call. I feel they must, and that is the reason I want to help in the prompting and encouraging. I say, O God teach me how to do it so we can get two to one or even more.

There are so many souls dropping out in the darkness, and the time is galloping on at such a rapid rate of speed that I feel the very fastest that we can work at our job of soul saving is too slow. There they go like a million a day before we can get to them. How to speed up the operation of our machinery is the puzzling question—how to cut loose the band that holds the bow bent to let the arrow fly—how to break the chain that holds the spring that cannot operate as long as it is bound—how to cut the bands that are preventing some of our members so we cannot yet declare ourselves "every member a worker." We must know how to operate the floodgates so the flood waters can rush down the channel and whirl the wheels a little faster. Oh, I feel that we must make one long hard dash after the souls of men and get them, and never stop till the work is completed. This can be done with every member a worker and all of our machinery in perfect operation at high speed.

I want to urge the pastors to keep on stirring up their members until they will know they are all putting their energy into operation to keep all of the Church activities in constant operation. Pastors should keep the W. M. B. sisters encouraged to put their very best into their work. They should also keep vigil over the V. L. B. young people so they can raise the free literature fund to an abounding height. There is scarcely any limit to the energy there is in young people. All of it should be harnessed up for use in our Church activities. I feel like this must be done. Men have succeeded in harnessing steam, water, electricity and gasoline so they are mighty forces to carry on business in the world. We must succeed in harnessing all the energy there is in every member of the Church and millions more that are to become members. I believe God is going to help us do it. It is too much for millions of heathen and sinners to be lost just because so much powerful energy is lying dormant instead of being in action. I say, O God give us wisdom and the favor of men in our efforts to gain souls. I wish everyone of our members, and especially the ministers, could read and comprehend this statement. I am afraid sometimes, as I review the situation, that our people do not realize the value of every minute. Every minute spent in some other way different from God's way as marked out by the Bible is not only lost to the one who does it, but how many souls are lost because these minutes are not used as they should or could be? Is this view too close? Does it put the pressure on too tight? How can it when souls are so valuable and so many are dropping into hell because so many of our minutes are lost?